TROPICAL
RAINFORESTS
of the World

TROPICAL
RAINFORESTS
of the World

TED SMART

This edition produced by Ted Smart for
The Book People Ltd,
Guardian House,
Godalming, Surrey GU7 2AE

ISBN 1-85613-018-5

Manufactured in Spain

Produced by : Ted Smart
Author : Rupert Matthews
Designed by : Sara Cooper
Photo Research by : Annie Price
Production Assistant : Seni Glaister

**The publishers wish to thank Survival Anglia
and Heather Angel and the staff of her
photographic library, Biophotos, for their
help and co-operation during the making of this
book and for allowing their photographs to be reproduced**

Fifty years ago the rain forest was called Green Hell, a place of eternal twilight, disease and death. A place all civilized men avoided at all costs. Today it is considered to be Nature's Wonderland, a place where conservation should be the first priority and the balance of nature is at its highest development. But the rain forest has not changed. It is still covered by green twilight, still a place of discomfort, and the beauty was always there. So if the forest has not changed, what has? Simply the attitudes of the humans who visit the great forests.

Nowhere are these changes more apparent than in the Amazon Basin of South America. Fifty years ago the vast Amazonian rain forest covered nearly half the continent and was virtually unexplored. Few outsiders pushed upriver and of those who did few enjoyed the experience. Just before the First World War a team of 50 Germans traveled into the headwaters of the Rio Beni to establish what lay in the utterly unknown region. Only 20 came out alive.

Today, modern medicines have made rain forest exploration a much less hazardous affair. Many naturalists actually enjoy pushing through remote regions to discover new species of plant or animal or to check on the numbers of those faced with extinction. But these modern travelers have the advantages of two-way radio, air support and effective medical aid.

In the old days the only worthwhile reason to penetrate to the interior was to gather rubber, but the average life of a rubber collector was incredibly short. A visiting European estimated that at any one time 9 out of 10 humans in the rain forest were suffering from a disease of some kind, mostly serious. Only those on the run from civilization, or those held in bondage, spent much time in the rain forest. Their sole escape from misery was the raw cane alcohol known as kachasa, which merely hastened their almost certain early death.

The few surveyors and explorers who traveled to the region brought with them well equipped expeditions and adequate supplies, but even they were not immune to the perils of the rain forest. Several expeditions vanished without trace, while one Scottish traveler lost his entire team and spent the rest of his short life as war leader of one of the wilder tribes. A second was held prisoner for many years because of his medical knowledge. He died of old age before any European expedition could

Top right: The treefrog Hyla boans photographed in Trinidad's Arima Valley. Above left: A leaf cutting ant (Atta) from Trinidad snipping free a section of leaf before carrying it back to the nest. The leaves are not consumed by the ants, but are laid in underground galleries and mixed with fungus spores. The fungus grows on the decomposing leaves and is then harvested by worker ants which pass it on to the rest of the nest. Above right: A view of the jaws of a whip scorpion, common in Caribbean rain forests. Left: A female harlequin beetle (Acrocinus longimanus) rests on a fallen tree in the Arima Valley.

reach him.

The dangers which accounted for so many lives were not as obvious as one might imagine. The jaguar many of which prowled through the forests in those days is a powerful cat every bit as strong and voracious as the lion or tiger. But though it occasionally took human prey, the jaguar was not a great danger and rarely took to maneating as did the Indian tiger. The dangers to humans in the rain

forest were, for the most part more subtle and insidious.

The rain forest contains some of the most diverse insect life in the world, and it was this which struck at most outsiders. Mosquitos and other species of blood-sucking flies swarmed through the air. In some areas the clouds of flies were so dense that it was impossible to speak or breathe without sucking in a mouthful of insects.

The constant attacks of these tiny creatures spread diseases such as malaria which claimed many lives.

More debilitating was the constant drain of blood and the continual skin irritation which reduced many people to listlessness and apathy. Sand-flies were small enough to go unnoticed until they bit, producing a sensation like a prick from a red-hot needle. Such attacks were all the more serious because of the lack of medicines or effective treatment. The bites itch but are liable to turn septic if scratched. In those days of long treks on foot even the best equipped expedition was liable to run out of medicines, and then there was nothing to stop infection. It was said that a man from the rain forest could be recognised by the sores, scabs and scars which covered his entire body.

Extremely unpleasant was a little grub called the sututu. This insect lays its eggs beneath the skin of a human or other mammal. The egg then hatches and the larva begins to develop. As it grows, the grub builds itself a cyst which produces a large inflamed area of skin. In the days before modern medicine there was little which could be done about the sututu. It could be killed with tobacco juice or alcohol, but that left it beneath the skin and led to a festering sore as the insect decomposed. Blood poisoning could result from such treatment, and without medicine that was usually fatal.

The only relief possible was to wait until the cyst was 'ripe', when the grub enlarged its breathing hole. This involved an agonizing wait of many days. The patient then had to watch patiently for the grub to poke its head out of the hole. Quick finger pressure on either side of the inflammation caused

Top: A variegated gecko from Trinidad. Left: A damselfly photograhed in the dense rain forest of the Arima Valley in Trinidad. Above: The small but colorful rain forest flowers of the Gesneria *genus. Flowers are an ever present part of the rain forest. With few differences between the seasons, plants may flower and fruit at any time of the year.*

the grub to pop out. Many long-suffering victims found great pleasure in grinding the now helpless larva beneath their boots.

Night brought no relief, for the blood-sucking insects were simply replaced by a fresh wave of night-flying insects. Mosquito nets were essential equipment for any expedition pushing upriver. Without them no outsider could have enjoyed an uninterrupted night's sleep. There were, however, other night parasites that the mosquito nets could not defeat.

Many regions of the forest are home to vampire bats. These creatures are generally no bigger than the palm of a man's hand, but can be persistent parasites. The bats fly silently and are attracted by the sound of a sleeping mammal. Landing on the

ground a short distance from their victim, the bats creep forwards on all fours. Reaching the intended victim the bats nip any exposed piece of skin with their extremely sharp canines. The tongue is then brought into play to lap up the oozing blood. The saliva contains a chemical which inhibits clotting and ensures a free flow of blood.

Early explorers suffered agonies from the vampire bats. The bats used their teeth to bite their way through the mosquito nets, which action at once allowed insects to enter. The only effective

defence in areas where the bats were known to be common was to wear thick shirts, trousers and scarves. Such protective clothing was effective, but terribly uncomfortable in the humid heat of the rain forests.

More unpleasant creatures lurked in the waters in the shape of a fish called the candiru. This insidious little creature is, thankfully, restricted to certain rivers but where present is a continual danger. It would appear to have an insatiable appetite for urea, a liking it will go to great lengths to indulge. Any person rash enough to enter a river infested with candiru would soon have had reason to regret it. The fish were said to be able to detect urine from a great distance and swim upstream to reach its source. The lucky victims received a small, but extremely painful bite on a tender part of their anatomy. Those more unfortunate found the tiny eel-like fish burrowing deep into their orifice. Immediate and drastic surgery was the only cure. When most men were their own doctors the candiru could be an extremely painful, and sometimes fatal, visitor.

Better known as a danger in the rivers are still the piranha. These tiny fish swim in great shoals and are famed for their voracious appetites and ability to strip a large creature of meat in seconds. The most dangerous species is the black piranha which grows to about 8 inches (10 cm) in length and may be found in shoals over a thousand strong. They prey mostly on large fish, but will readily attack any creature within reach. Their sense of

smell is quite extraordinary, and they can detect minute traces of blood in the river. Once blood flows from a creature in the water, the piranha feed frenziedly. A creature as large as a horse can be torn to pieces in under a minute.

The liking for blood has made the piranha particularly dangerous near villages and towns. Blood from slaughterhouses sets the fish in a perpetual feeding frenzy and they are likely to attack anything which moves. Numerous tales have been told of the piranha, some perhaps containing more exaggeration than truth. One tells of a butcher who slipped into the Rio Miranda after depositing a bucket of offal. He did not even have time to surface before the piranha had killed him.

Larger and equally deadly creatures lurk in the rivers. The anaconda is a giant constricting snake which swims through the larger rivers and swamps in search of prey. Its favorite trick is suddenly to

emerge from the depths at places where game drink and seize anything within reach. It kills by looping its body around that of the victim and slowly suffocating it. The exact size of these huge snakes is not certain. The largest specimen to be brought out the forests and measured was about 30 feet (10 meters) long. Reputable early explorers have on several occasions reported snakes twice that length while less reliable sources speak of monsters over 100 feet (30 meters) long.

A potentially reliable tale of the giant snake dates from 1947 when a party of Brazilian officials and soldiers marched deep in to the forests in an attempt to patch up a peace treaty with the Chaventes tribe which had begun killing rubber tappers. One of the men on the team was an artist named Bonacase who was asked to sketch anything of interest. When hunting for capybara, one of the soldiers came across a massive snake and shot it

Previous pages: Bromeliads growing on a tree branch high in the canopy in Trinidad. These plants root on trees, but are not parasitic. These pages: The jaguar is the largest and most formidable cat of the New World rain forests. It ranges from southern Mexico to Argentina. Though it will take fish and lizards, the jaguar prefers large mammals. Peccaries are a favored prey, as are deer and tapir. It has almost disappeared from open plains, but remains in the rain forests.

Facing page: Epiphytic plants. Above: A robber fly (Asilidae). Above right: A coatimundi (Nasua nasua). Right: A lanternwing insect, Panama. Below: South American bullfrog. Overleaf: (main picture) The Arima Valley; (top left) tapir (Tapirus bairdi); (bottom right) red squirrel (Sciurus granatensis); (bottom center) colorful Erythrina from Panama; (bottom right) the blooms of the vine Clitorea from Panama.

several times.

Bonacase wanted to know how big the snake was, although his companions did not treat the monster as at all unusual. He cut a piece of string to the length from his finger tips to the opposite shoulder, a distance he reckoned at around 3 feet (90 centimeters). He found the snake was 25 times as long as the string and one and a half times as long around the middle. This would mean the snake was some 75 feet (23 meters) long and 4 feet (1.4 meters) around. It proved impossible to carry either the entire skin or the skull in addition to the official stores so the carcass was left. Inevitably the lack of hard evidence led to the story being entirely disbelieved.

Whatever their size, the anaconda has entered the folklore of the river. It is rumored that the eyes of the anaconda glow at night with a cold, blue fire eerily attractive and fascinating which lures the unwary to their deaths. In some areas the snakes are termed 'sleepers' for their deep regular breathing sounds like gentle snoring. Elsewhere the breathing is feared for it is said to paralyse potential victims.

Nor were the dangers and discomforts of the Green Hell restricted to the animals and plants of the great forests. Death could come from human hands as effectively and silently as from natural causes. Some of the native tribes were friendly to travelers, but others were likely to eat visitors and some were inclined to treat any stranger as an enemy. It was not at all unusual for a boat carrying an exploration team to be met by a shower of arrows as it rounded a bend in the river. A favorite trick of the tribesmen was to creep up on a camp at dawn and shower the mosquito nets with arrows. One expedition suffered so many such attacks that the men took to sleeping under bushes some distance from the mosquito nets. They preferred to brave the insects rather than the deadly arrows.

The tribesmen were formidable enemies. The arrows they used were accurate over a distance of more than a hundred yards and were propelled with great force. They could easily penetrate through the body of a man. Even if they inflicted only light wounds, the arrows could deal out death for they were often tipped with deadly poison. Or in the heat and damp the wounds could turn septic and lead to blood-poisoning.

The favored tactics of the Amazonian Indians were those of ambush and surprise. A volley of arrows or blowdarts would erupt from the foliage, then silence would ensue as the Indians made their escape. Repeated attacks of this kind could destroy even the largest expedition and probably accounted for many of the smaller teams which vanished in the interior.

The fighting was not all one way. The intruders from civilization invariably carried guns and most would not hesitate to use them when attacked. Some of the rubber managers launched slave raids on tribal villages to gain forced recruits to their dwindling workforce. Such raids could be extremely savage. Entire villages were destroyed, the able-bodied young adults enslaved and the rest slaughtered. Ignorance led to further bloodshed for settlers who had suffered an Indian attack tended to retaliate against the nearest tribe, even if had not been involved.

In the past the rain forest truly deserved its name of Green Hell. It was an uncomfortable, dangerous and violent place where sudden death or long suffering were the constant companions of

anyone who ventured into the deep unknown. Even those most accustomed to the rain forest could not expect to escape unscathed. Colonel Percy Fawcett spent many years in the interior tracing rivers and mapping regions on behalf of various governments. In 1925 Fawcett, his son Jack and a friend named Raleigh set off from Cuyaba on a route which would take them down the Rio Xingu across the Sierra Estrondo and so through unexplored country to Bahia, a journey of some 1500 miles (2700 km). After two years he

captive by a tribe called Aruvudu many weeks journey away. She said the men could not escape because they had run out of bullets for their guns. The descriptions she gave closely fitted Fawcett and the others. A rescue team was organized, but after several weeks journey it ran into a full scale tribal war and was forced to turn back. Nothing more was ever heard of Fawcett.

It might be wondered why anybody bothered to intrude into such an unpleasant place, but the Green Hell had its attractions as well as its

*Right: Lowland rain forest steams after heavy rain. Left: An anolis lizard (*Anolis frenatus*). Below: Mating frogs of the genus* Shilisca. *Bottom: Pike-headed vine snake (*Oxybelis aeneus*) of Central America. Facing page: Red-eyed treefrog (*Agalychnis*). Overleaf: Monte Verde in Costa Rica.*

had failed to emerge and concern mounted.

Because Fawcett was so well known his disappearance led to much interest and several expeditions were launched into the interior to try to discover his fate. In 1928 a team traced Fawcett's route as far as the Kuluene River and a village of the Kalapalo tribe. The chief confirmed that a trio of white men accompanied by mules had passed through about three years earlier. He reported the men had continued eastwards and added that the smoke from the camp fires had been seen for five days as they gradually moved further away. Tribes further east denied ever having seen Fawcett. Suspicions grew that they had killed Fawcett for some reason, or at least that he had died among them. In 1930 a second team reached the Kalapalos and moved east, never to be seen again.

In 1932 a Swiss named Rattin set out to follow up reports of white captives being held by Indians. He too vanished without trace. The following year an Indian woman arrived at a ranch searching for work. She told of three white men being held

unpleasantness. One explorer returning to the rain forest in 1935 on an expedition which was nearly to cost him his life, wrote to a friend. 'I must go back. Perhaps it is hard to understand. We went through much misery, but I must go back, even if I go alone.' Many other early travelers spoke of the strange lure of the rain forest. One remarked that as soon as he entered the forest he longed to leave, but once back in civilization he felt an irresistible impulse to return to the forests.

For Fawcett and others like him there was the eternal lure of exploration, the chance of discovering something nobody had seen before. In the days before aircraft became common, nobody knew how far the rain forest extended nor what lay beyond the next hill. Stories and rumors abounded as to what existed deep in the interior.

Perhaps the most attractive tales were those which concerned lost treasures. It was a well-known historical fact that the Incas found much silver in the eastern foothills of the Andes. Also undoubtedly true was that early Spanish adventurers had found several abandoned silver mines in the

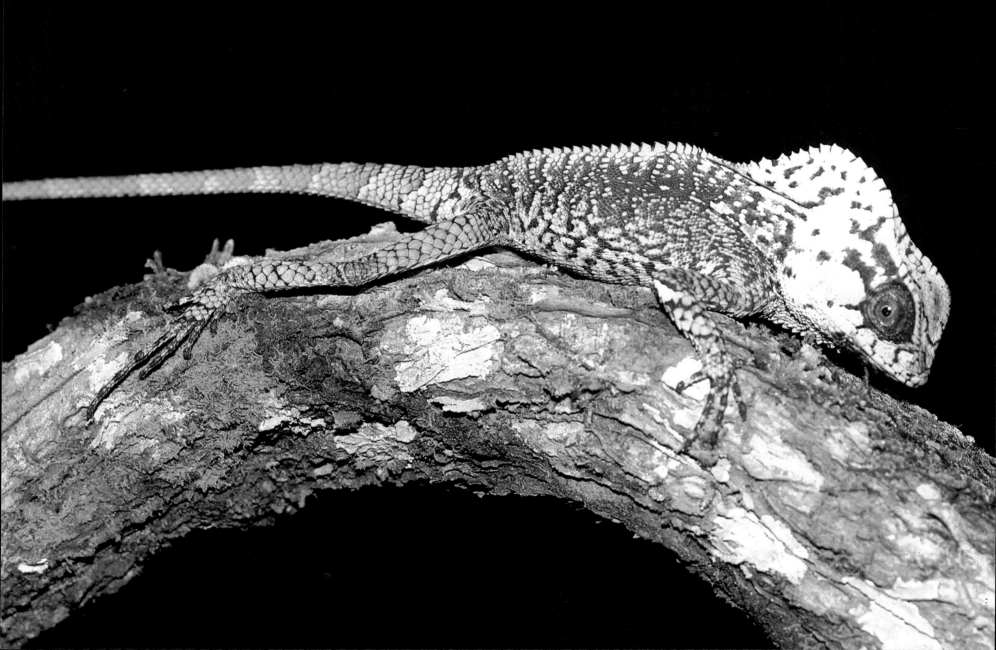

same area. Tales of rediscovered lost mines were common and lured many into the forested foothills.

Other treasure stories concerned rivers with beds studded with gold nuggets or with diamonds. Such tales were not unbelievable and several prospectors made a living by grubbing gold from forest streams. Some more competent mineralogists made tidy fortunes and were able to retire with enough cash to live on for life. The wealth-bearing streams tended to be concentrated in the mountains which fringe the great Amazon basin though the upland rain forest blanketed the hills and shaded the rich rivers it was a forest different in character from the hot, humid, stifling rain forest of

Facing page: (top) the head of the basilisk Basiliscus americana *and (bottom) a helmeted iguana (*Coryptophanes cristatus*) of Central America. Below: The livid green of polychrus. Right: A slender lizard on a leaf in Costa Rica. Bottom: An* Anolis *lizard. Overleaf: A coiled boa constrictor.*

the lowlands.

Perhaps the most persistent rumors of the lowlands concerned ruined towns and cities. Deep in the unexplored forests, it was said, there were vast ruins of massive stone blocks overgrown by jungle and tumbled to the ground. In the 1740s a Portuguese settler stumbled out of the rain forest with a remarkable tale. He said he had come across a ruined city arranged around a great open square dominated by a large statue. He added that the largest building had been approached by a flight of steps and was covered with carvings. The city was big enough to have housed many thousands but must have been abandoned for many generations for it was a complete ruin and densely overgrown. The account was filed in government records and then forgotten until the early 20th century when it was rediscovered and published.

Meanwhile other stories of ruined cities had been filtering out of the forests. Sometimes the rumors could not be pinned down, but occasionally a person actually claimed to have seen the ruins

*Left: An orange tree frog (*Bojo peregienes*). Far left top: The tree frog* Agalychnis spurrelli. *Far left bottom: The poison tree frog (*Hyla ebbraccata*). Below: The flaming arrow poison frog (*Dendrobates pumilio*) of Costa Rica. Local tribesmen tip their arrows with poison which is extracted from the skin of this frog by roasting it over a fire. Facing page top: A female litter frog (*Eleutherodactylus bransfordi*) of Central America. Facing page bottom:* Hyla boulanger.

for himself. Inevitably the ruins were said to be many weeks journey distant and very difficult to reach. In some reports treasure was said to be located in the ruins.

White Indians were another favorite topic of rumor and legend. On several occasions travelers claimed to have seen, or even conversed with, tribes of clearly European appearance. Exactly who these 'white Indians' were and where they came from remained shrouded in mystery.

By the early 1920s the various stories had been brought together and woven into a remarkable theory. The actual discovery of lost cities in the Andes added to the debate and lent credence to the reports from the Amazon. At that time archaeology had revealed little about pre-Columbian history and almost anything could be believed.

It was thought that many thousands of years earlier a massive and powerful civilization had

grown up in the interior. Some claimed it was connected with Atlantis, perhaps having been established by refugees from the drowning nation. Some hundreds of years ago the civilization entered decline, due to natural disasters and civil war. The cities were abandoned and the survivors fled to inaccessible forest areas. There they ringed themselves with warlike tribes who were paid with food and tools to keep outsiders at a distance. Many explorers thought that some such chain of events might explain the ruined cities and 'white Indians' reported with such regularity. Certainly Colonel Fawcett held this view. He was searching for the remnant population of the civilization when he vanished.

In 1935 William La Varre, a fellow of the Royal Geographical Society, made definite contact with the Waiwai tribe which was characterized by light skin and aquiline features. They lived in an isolated valley of the Akarai Mountains of British Guiana. Disappointingly for the romantic legends, the tribe

Left: The tree snake (Corallus annulatus). Below left: A colubrid tree snake. Below: A pike-headed vine snake (Oxybelis aeneus). Several species of vine snake inhabit the rain forest of Central America where they hunt lizards and young birds. Facing page: Aloreate parrot snake (Leptophis nebulosus) showing its threat display used against rivals. Overleaf: (main picture) highland rain forest in Costa Rica; (top left) a forest iguana (Polychrus) which lies on twigs awaiting passing insects which it can snap up; (bottom left) a male harlequin frog (Atelopus varius); top right: a helmet lizard (Corytophanes cristatus); (bottom right) a poison frog of the genus Dendrobates. Tree frogs such as this lay eggs in the pools of water which collect in hollow trunks or where branches fork.

Facing page: Cloud forest on the aptly named Monte Verde, in Costa Rica. Monte Verde translates as 'green mountain'.

Cloud forest is a specific type of rain forest which occurs at high altitude where low clouds encase the forest in near perpetual fog.

Undergrowth flourishes in the damp atmosphere. Top: A pale green snake of the Leptophis *genus. Above: Schlegel's viper*

(Bothrops schlegii) *is a pit viper with an unusual hunting technique. The snake frequents the canopy, spending most of its*

time coiled on a branch with its tail firmly wrapped around the tree for support. When a bird flies within reach, the snake strikes,

lunging forward. After the strike it is left dangling by its tail until it draws itself back up to the branch where the victim is devoured.

had a culture exactly similar to that of their neighbors. But there still remained the mystic lure of the unknown, of the possibility that 'white Indians' inhabiting magnificent cities existed in some as-yet undiscovered valley. Not until the great rain forest was regularly criss-crossed by aircraft did the legend finally die.

One strange legend which did prove to have a basis in fact was that of the Amazons, from which the great river took its name. The original Amazons were legendary women warriors which the ancient Greeks believed lived near the Caucasus Mountains. It was said that the Amazons lived without men, but occasionally invited men to their village for mating purposes. The Amazon River gained its name in 1541 when the first Spanish explorers to drift down the waterway from the Andes to the Atlantic found themselves under attack. Led by Orellana, a friend of Pizarro who had conquered the Incas in the Andes, the Spaniards fought off the attack. The bowmen, they declared, were women and no men were visible. In fact, the warriors were almost certainly men. Later travelers noted the fact that some tribes were distinguished by feminine features and long dress-like clothing.

Over the following years the tales of female warriors and villages full of women continued to leak out of the great forests. As with the tales of lost cities, opinion was seriously divided between those who thought anything possible in the Amazon rain forest and those who discounted such fanciful stories.

Then, in the 1930s, came confirmation of the tales. A team of geologists searching for diamonds encountered a group of Indians traveling to a village famed for the excellence of its poison. They

carried small colored stones to exchange for poison. The stones, they said, were invitations from the 'village of women who live alone'. Intrigued the expedition visited the village to find that it was, indeed, composed entirely of women and children. The explanation was that the women came from a nearby tribe, but were banished to live on their own until they had produced a male child. They were then considered to be of use to the tribe and were allowed to return to their home villages. Having discovered the secret of the 'village of women who live alone', the team found great difficulty in persuading their porters to leave the place. Several later deserted to return to the women.

Hardly had the lure of lost cities and unknown civilizations died than a new attraction beckoned travelers to the Green Hell. It was a fascination which would transform the public perception of the rain forest from Green Hell to Green Heaven.

In short the change came about because people in general became increasingly interested in the natural world. Before long it was realized that the rain forests contained more species than any other habitat. There are certainly many thousands of insect species as yet unknown to science, and mysterious tales of larger creatures continually

Top: Atelopus varius. *Above:* Hyla ebracatta. *Above right: The species* callidrya. *Right: A tiny* Eleutherodactylus diastema. *Facing page: (top) a female harlequin frog of the* Atelopus varius *and (bottom) a pair of* Agalychnis callidryas *laying eggs. Several species of tree frog lay their eggs in froth on leaves, transferring the*

tadpoles to water as they hatch. Overleaf: (top left) a hummingbird on its nest; (bottom left) hummingbird chicks; (right) tree ferns in the cloud forest.

filter out of the interior. It has been estimated that around 40% of living species live in rain forests.

The animals of the rain forest shed their old image of being either edible or dangerous and became fascinating in their own right. Numerous scientific teams moved into the forest to study the wildlife. Many took with them film cameras to record the extraordinary collection of creatures which they found and the forest itself. The films and television programmes produced by this scientific activity spurred public interest even more. Film producers descended on the rain forest in increasing numbers, accompanied by more studious teams intent on unraveling the secrets of the incredibly diverse environment.

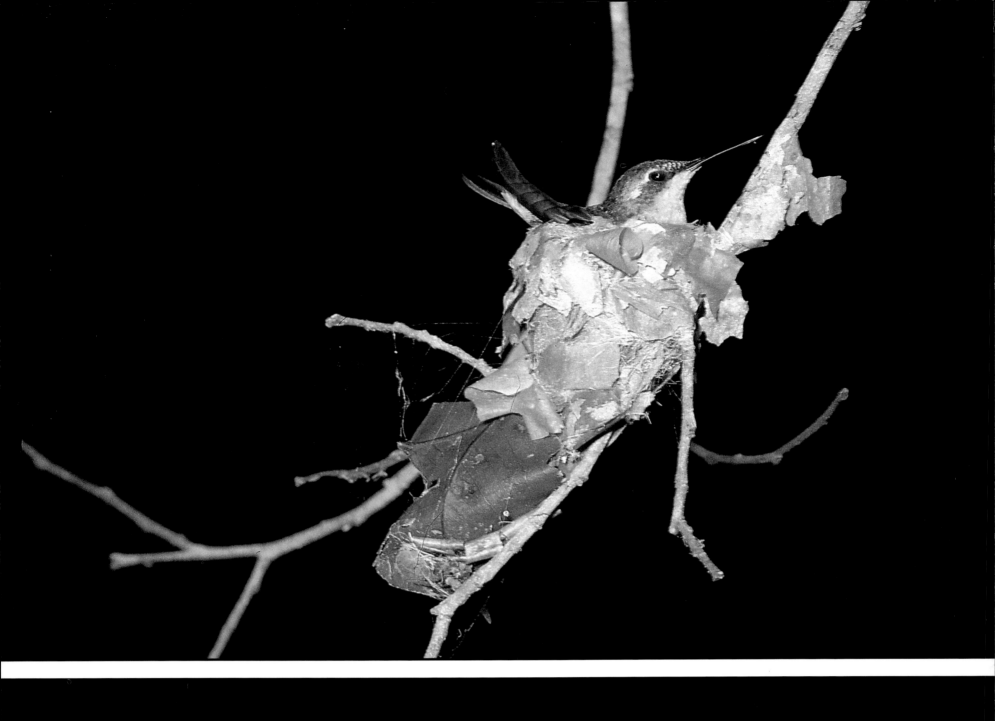

*Facing page: A network of aerial roots descend from a forest giant as epiphytic plants push down in the search for water and nutrients from the soil. Right: The eyelash viper (*Bothrops sp.*), a bird eating pit viper which frequents the canopy of Central American rain forests. Below: A cribo snake (*Drymarchon corais) searching for prey in the leaf litter on the forest floor. Below right:* Bothrops nasutus. *Several species of the genus* Bothrops *inhabit the rain forests of the New World. Like all pit vipers, these snakes are highly venomous and are able to kill their prey with a single bite. Their victims are found not only by sight and smell, but also by heat. Two small pits in the viper's head are capable of detecting the direction and size of a heat source.*

What they found was a surprising contrast between the apparent richness of the rain forest and its actual poverty. The incongruous nature of the rain forest is that although it supports one of the richest faunas and floras on earth, it is starved of nutrients and fertility. The fact that such contrasts can exist is explained by the incredible nature of the rain forest itself.

Rain forest is a complicated tropical ecosystem which covers vast areas of the world in the tropics. The climate of the rain forest is particularly distinctive. It is dominated by high temperatures and heavy rainfall. The air is generally between 70 and 90 degrees fahrenheit (20 and 30 degrees centigrade) throughout the year while as much as 1600 inches (4,000 mm) of rain may fall in a year.

There is little difference between the seasons. A day at any time of the year is likely to be about the same temperature and to experience about the same amount of rainfall as any other.

It is mainly the constant climate which accounts for the rapid growth in a rain forest. All living things need warmth, water and food in order to grow and the rain forest contains the first two in abundance. No other ecosystem is capable of sustaining such rapid and spectacular growth. Any plant or animal which dies falls to the forest floor where it is at once attacked by fungi, insects and other detritus feeders. Within a matter of days any organic matter is broken down into its constituent parts and disappears. Only the largest trees survive longer once they are fallen. Even they remain as features

for only a few months. The inside of the trunk is penetrated by termites and insects which rapidly excavate the interior. Many human travelers have been surprised when sitting or leaning on an apparently solid logs to find them collapse under their weight.

It is this rapid turnover of nutrients and organic chemicals which enables the rain forest to exist. The actual amount of nutrients is surprisingly low, certainly less than in temperate forests. Because it is recycled so quickly due to the heat and humidity, the material can be absorbed by other plants and used to produce fresh growth. Indeed the fertile compost-like layer in a rain forest soil is rarely more than a few inches deep. Beneath that the soil is poor, heavily leached and highly infertile. The

lush growth of the rain forest is deceptive, and has led to some fatal misunderstandings.

The native tribes which inhabit the Amazonian rain forest live largely from the forest itself. Before the Europeans penetrated the forests in large numbers, the native tribes hunted forest creatures and gathered fruits and leaves from wild plants. What agriculture did take place was at a very low level for the rain forest supplied most of what was needed.

When Europeans or European-influenced locals attempted to clear large patches of rain forest for agriculture they quickly found that the land was not as fertile as it seemed. Accustomed to temperate forests which could be cleared to produce highly fertile farmland, the newcomers were puzzled. A freshly cleared patch of land produced rich crops for a year or two, but then the land failed. What was happening was that the few nutrients, which the rain forest had constantly recycled, were being removed by harvesting of the crops and not replaced by fertilizer or manure. The only option open to farmers was to move on to a fresh section of rain forest and begin again.

Prior to this century such a pattern was repeated endlessly around the fringes of the rain forest. Patches were cleared, farmed and then abandoned. Within a few years the rain forest re-established itself as seeds from the surrounding trees were brought into the clearing and germinated. The climate of the rain forest and its inherent vitality ensured that small clearings quickly regenerated to forest.

When large scale clearances take place, however, no such regeneration is possible. The rain forest, it has been discovered, is not only possible because of the climate, it largely creates the climate itself. The massive leaf area in the forest and the heat ensures that large quantities of

moisture are released into the atmosphere every day. This rises until it condenses out into clouds and then rain to return to the ground and be taken up by the plants again.

When the trees are cut down over a large area the cycle of rainfall and evaporation is broken. The air loses its humidity and the rain ceases to fall. The land dries out to become arid semi-desert suitable only for rough pasture. Once the chain of nutrient and water recycling is broken it is very

difficult, if not impossible, for it to re-establish itself. Despite its apparent vitality and fertility, the rain forest is a delicate environment.

In the undisturbed rain forest, the pattern of life is dominated by the trees which are the dominant flora. It is the trees which provide the most visible aspect of the rain forest and which supply the vast majority of habitats for life. There are a great many species of tree in the Amazon, but most have a common pattern of growth.

*Facing page: A bare-throated tiger-heron (*Tigrisoma mexicanum*). Top: A pair of Guatemalan howler monkeys (*Alouatta villosa*), the only jet black howlers. This species is restricted to a small area of upland forest in Central America where it inhabits the damp, misty rain forest properly referred to as cloud forest. Left: A woolly opossum (*Caluromys laniger*). Opossums are the only marsupials to live outside Australasia and are restricted to the New World. Above: A pair of Baird's tapirs (*Tapirus bairdi*) resting in a rain forest pool in Central America. This rare creature is active chiefly at night, spending the days at rest in streams, pools or dense thickets.*

Previous pages: Two views of the Costa Rican cloud forest. Left: A wolf spider awaits the chance to strike. Below: A tegnaria spider from Central America. Bottom left: A katydid shedding its skin, the katydid is a relative of the grasshoppers. Bottom right: A web-throwing spider prepares to launch its net-like web at a victim. Facing page: (top) A hunting spider and (bottom) a well-camouflaged katydid. Overleaf: (left) a tree with stilt roots; (top right) an epidendrum orchid and (bottom right) a colorful Liliaceae.

The mature trees stand some 100 feet (30 meters) tall and consist of tall, straight trunks which spread out near the top into a broad umbrella of branches and twigs all of which are covered with leaves. The dense network of branches and leaves is designed to grab as much sunlight as possible. So successful is the structure that it absorbs some 98% of light, leaving the forest floor in a perpetual twilight.

Seen from above the rain forest appears as an unbroken carpet of greenery. This is made up of the dense foliage of the trees which are packed tightly together to grasp every chance of absorbing light. The solid blanket of leaves is generally known as the canopy and stretches unbroken for

thousands of miles in the Amazon.

But the apparent uniformity is deceptive. Many trees exhibit what is known as 'canopy shyness'. This means that the outermost branches and twigs do not actually touch those of the neighboring tree, leaving narrow spaces between the two. Nobody is entirely certain why this canopy shyness occurs, nor how the trees regulate the gap between themselves. It has been suggested, however, that it is a defence mechanism against parasites. The gap, though small, makes it difficult for insect larvae and other wood-boring creatures to cross from one tree to another.

The uniform canopy is also occasionally broken by overlarge trees which may grow 30 feet (10 meters) or more above the other trees. These giants tower above the canopy as normal trees grow from the ground. They spread their branches into the light untroubled either by canopy shyness or other plants competing for space.

In the struggle for light only those plants capable of reaching the canopy can survive. Young plants have a serious problem getting established. In fact of the many thousands of seeds produced by rain forest trees very few ever grow to maturity. The vast majority are consumed before they can fall to the ground by the creatures which throng the canopy. Those seeds that do reach the forest floor are often attacked by insects or mammals which devour them eagerly.

Those that remain intact long enough to germinate are immediately faced with the problem of finding enough light to photosynthesise and therefore survive. The forest floor is not only dim but is starved of the light frequencies vital for photosynthesis by the dense canopy above. Seedlings rarely flourish and most die young. Only when an adult tree dies and crashes to the ground is light able to penetrate to the forest floor and so provide the young trees with nourishment.

When such a gap occurs in the canopy, the sunlit patch of ground bursts forth in a rapid race of growth. Seedlings shoot upward in an attempt to beat others to the life-giving sunlight while undergrowth flourishes for a brief span. One of the trees eventually succeeds in reaching the canopy and shuts off the light which had provided the incentive

for the burst of growth.

The difficulties faced by trees in the rain forest do not stop with that faced by saplings. Adult trees, too need to be able to cope with the difficult conditions. One of the most critical of these is the problem of staying upright. The soil in rain forests is typically shallow and sandy. A 100 foot (30 meter) tall tree weighing many tons may grow from distinctly unstable foundations. The surrounding trees give some support and protect the tree from high winds, but with a normal root system the plant would still be in danger of collapse. Many rain forest species therefore have great flaring buttresses which spread out around its base. These serve to expand the base of the tree and give greater stability to the trunk.

In the canopy the trees must face the problem of heavy and frequent downpours of rain in which many inches of rain may fall in a few minutes. Such massive torrents of water are liable to batter

leaves from twigs and may encourage rot if allowed to collect. Most trees have therefore long, pointed leaves which are shaped so as to bend under the pressure of heavy rainfall and to channel the water downward toward the roots.

Many plants in the rain forest have avoided the need to race for the sunlight in this way by evolving other growth patterns. The creepers are often the most noticeable in a patch of forest. These plants germinate on the forest floor and rapidly produce a small, flat patch of leaves. From this center long tendrils snake out across the ground until they reach a vertical support, which in the rain forest is almost always a tree trunk. Up these the tendrils

squirm, hooking into crevices in the bark and securing their hold as they climb.

As soon as the stem reaches a patch of sunlight, it bursts forth into a dense mass of leaves and flowers in order to photosynthesise food and produce seeds. Fresh stems move on and up from the clump of leaves in a continual search for fresh areas of light. Clearly the most vulnerable part of any climber is its long trailing stem which may be hundreds of feet long. Any break in this long, thin lifeline would cause death to the part of the plant above that point. To protect themselves against hungry animals many of the climbers have evolved savage thorns capable of tearing through the flesh

The insect life of the rain forest is the most diverse and colorful section of the fauna, especially in Central America. Top left: The spotted butterfly Heliconius anderida *from Central America. Top right: A sphyngid moth from Costa Rica. Above left: An owl butterfly (*Caligo teucer*). The large spots*

*on the wings of this species are used to frighten predators. The Above: A tiny transparent winged butterfly (*Hypoleria*). Facing page top: A damselfly. Facing page bottom: A delicate clearwing butterfly (*Citherias menander*) caught in a spider's web in Costa Rica.*

of any creature unwise enough to approach too closely.

Other plants avoid the forest floor altogether and instead grow directly in the canopy. Some of these are parasites, but the majority are epiphytes, which do little harm to the tree on which they grow. Because of the almost interminable rain which deluges the rain forest year round any crevice or fork in a tree is inevitably damp and moist. Seeds which fall here find ideal conditions to germinate and start growth. As the seedlings struggle to find the light, they use their aerial roots to absorb moisture from the rain and to anchor themselves more securely to the host. The upper branches of the trees are festooned with ferns and orchids, shrubs and creepers.

One of the most dramatic epiphytes is the strangling fig which is especially common in the Amazonian rain forest. This flamboyant plant took its name from its curious growing habits. It begins life much like any other epiphyte by sprouting in a

Left: A bosleria orchid Above: The tiny purple flowers of a wild fuchsia. Below left: A lobelia type flower found in the cloud forest of Monte Verde in Costa Rica. Below: The aroid plant. Facing page: The bright red flowers of the amazonia plant. The flowers of the rain forest are particularly colorful as they need to attract insects amid a dense tangle of other plants and flowers.

damp crevice in a tall tree. As it grows, it pushes down long, strong aerial roots which snake around the trunk of the host tree on their way to the forest floor. Once they have made contact with the ground, the roots act like those of normal plants. They burrow into the soil extracting both moisture and nutrients. As the years pass the roots of the strangling fig become thicker and more robust until they are able to support the weight of the fig plant.

Sometimes the host tree dies as the strangling fig reaches such maturity. When this occurs the trunk rots and dies, leaving the tough lattice work of interconnected fig roots as the hollow trunk of a new tree every bit as large as the one-time host. It was once thought that the fig literally strangled its host, causing its premature death. It was reasoned that in this way the fig guaranteed itself a place in the canopy without having to risk the seed finding a patch of forest floor open to the sun.

This theory has now been seriously called into question. It has been pointed out that the fig neither penetrates the host tree nor does any noticeable damage to it. The only noticeable effect is that the trunk of the host is distorted and furrowed by the pressure of the fig roots. Occasionally a host tree outlives a strangling fig. Such trees are easily recognisable by the strange patterns which seem to have been gouged out of the bark.

If the strangling fig has lost some of its reputation for predatory behaviour, the same cannot be said of the insect-eating plants which abound in the Amazonian rain forests. The butterworts grow in damp, poor soil where nutrients are scarce and other plants have difficulty surviving. To gather more minerals than are available to its roots, the butterworts trap insects and dissolve their bodies.

The plant carries a bright flower and has glands on its shiny leaves which exude a sweet, yellowy substance. Flies and other insects are attracted to these and settle on the plant. If they are unfortunate enough to land on a leaf, the insects become glued to the surface. The struggles of the hapless animal stimulate the leaf into producing highly

acidic liquids which break down the softer parts of the creature into organic compounds which can be readily absorbed by the plant.

More spectacular are the pitcher plants which abound in various tropical habitats, including the rain forests. These plants produce special leaves which take the form of large jugs, or pitchers. The pitcher may have a capacity of anything up to 2 pints (1 liter) depending on the species. The top of the pitcher is generally covered by a 'lid' which prevents rain from swamping the delicate trap. Inside the pitcher is about one third full of digestive juices capable of breaking down tough insect bodies.

To tempt the insect into the deadly liquid, the pitcher plant exudes a sugary substance similar to nectar which forms a layer part way down the inside of the pitcher. As an insect climbs inside the pitcher and creeps down toward the sweet substance, it encounters a film of extremely slippery

Facing page: A black polistes wasp rests on the paper-thin walls of its nest in Costa Rica. Top right: A blackcurrant grasshopper rests on a leaf in Costa Rica. Above: A colony of yellow termites constructing a nest in the rain forest of Central America. Termites are ever present in the rain forests of the New World. Right: The reduvid bug of Corcovado in Central America.

scales on which it loses its footing and plunges headlong into the liquid at the base of the pitcher. Once in the digestive juices, the insect is doomed. It is too waterlogged to clamber out and the acids get to work almost at once.

A fascinating example of one species evolving to take advantage of another is that of the tiny red crab spider. This little creature has developed to survive within the pitcher. It is able to clamber over the slippery layer without harm and can even tolerate short immersions in the deadly fluids. It feeds by picking off insects before they tumble into the trap. As soon as a victim appears on the lip of the pitcher, attracted by the sweetness, the spider strikes. An active spider is capable of taking all insects which enter the pitcher, robbing the plant of its food. The plant is able to survive because it usually has several pitchers open as traps at any one time and it is unlikely that crab spiders will infest all of them simultaneously.

That some plants have the ability to kill insects has never been doubted, but in the early days of exploration of the rain forests more alarming tales seeped out to civilization. Wild stories sometimes reached remote posts of a tree called the ya-te-veo which was most often sighted in the northern forests of South America. The tree was said to have a squat trunk some 8 feet (2.5 meters) tall from which spread long tendrils across the forest floor. The edges of the tendrils, it was said, were lined with long, needle sharp spines.

When a creature stepped on these, the creepers whipped up in coils, gathering the intruder to the plants stem. As the tendrils writhed around the

victim the spines ripped into the flesh releasing a flow of blood which was caught in hollows in the stem. For ten days the tendrils remained locked around the victim. After this time they gradually relaxed to spread out again in wait for another victim. Only the bones of the victim were left to bear witness to its passing.

More ambitious story-tellers related that the plant was not only capable of taking rodents and tapirs but was even capable of capturing humans. Perhaps the most reliable account of such a plant came from a Mr Dunstan who was searching for insects when he had to rescue his dog from the clutches of the ya-te-veo in 1891. Despite much scientific investigation of the rain forest flora no such plant has ever been brought out of the rain forests for scientific examination.

However, the rain forest has always been full of surprises, and the fact that the man-eating tree is not scientifically recognised does not necessarily mean that it does not exist. One of the most outstanding biological riddles of the rain forest is that of the creatures universally known as 'Loys's ape'. For over 70 years this creature has been the subject of much scientific debate and its existence is still not universally accepted.

The story of this peculiar creature began in 1917 when Francois de Loys, a Swiss geologist, was exploring the rain forest around the headwaters of the Orinoco in western Venezuela. As with all explorers in those days, de Loys carried a rifle close to hand for protection against forest animals or local tribesmen. Suddenly he and his party found themselves confronted by a pair of 5 foot tall apes. The creatures clearly resented the intrusion. They screamed and leapt around before pelting the party with fruit and their own excrement. Like all scientific men, de Loys knew that apes did not live in South America. Whipping his rifle to his shoulder he shot one of the creatures which turned out to be female.

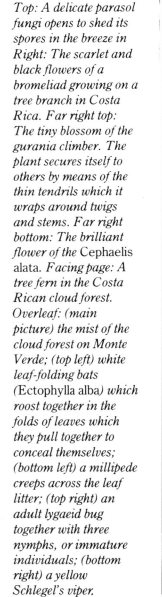

Top: A delicate parasol fungi opens to shed its spores in the breeze in Right: The scarlet and black flowers of a bromeliad growing on a tree branch in Costa Rica. Far right top: The tiny blossom of the gurania climber. The plant secures itself to others by means of the thin tendrils which it wraps around twigs and stems. Far right bottom: The brilliant flower of the Cephaelis alata. *Facing page: A tree fern in the Costa Rican cloud forest. Overleaf: (main picture) the mist of the cloud forest on Monte Verde; (top left) white leaf-folding bats* (Ectophylla alba) *which roost together in the folds of leaves which they pull together to conceal themselves; (bottom left) a millipede creeps across the leaf litter; (top right) an adult lygaeid bug together with three nymphs, or immature individuals; (bottom right) a yellow Schlegel's viper.*

Left: A yellow flower of the Acanthaceae *family, which is fairly widespread in South American rain forests. Above: The inconspicuous flowers of a creeper in the cloud forest of Central America. Below: A delicate white spike of flowers growing from a tree trunk. Below right: A cluster of epidendron orchids growing from a single stem. Facing page: A passion flower and ripening fruits. Because of the lack of distinct seasons in most rain forests, plants may produce fruits or simultaneously carry flowers and fruits for many months of the year.*

Left: The La Selva River in Costa Rica. The sluggish waters and crowding vegetation are typical of rain forest rivers which in many areas provide the only practical means of transport other than by air. Below left: The complex hangnests of the Montezuma oropendola which are woven so as to dangle beneath branches. As many as 100 nests may be found in one tree. Below: A passion flower of the Passiflora genus. Facing page: A densely forested slope. Overleaf: (main picture) rain forest around El Triunfo in Mexico; (top right) a roseatte spoonbill (Ajaia ajaja) which takes its name from the pinkish tinge to the feathers; (bottom near right) a roosting Chrotopterus bat; (bottom far right) a yellow headed parrot.

De Loys was many miles from civilization and he had no means of transporting the carcass through the stifling heat without it turning putrid. Hurriedly, de Loys made camp. Unlike many other travelers of the time de Loys carried photographic equipment with him. He photographed the strange beast and then took careful measurements and a detailed description. Next morning he moved on convinced that he had made a major scientific discovery.

Unfortunately nobody else agreed with him. When de Loys emerged from the rain forest some weeks later with his photo and measurements he was met with blank disbelief by the scientific world. The prevailing attitude seemed to be that since no apes were known from the New World, then no apes could exist. De Loys, it was suggested, might have been mistaken or might have been lying, but either way his claims could not be taken seriously. The undoubted existence of some large primate in the South American rain forest was allowed to slip

Above: Tropical sunset over the Rio Demini in northern Brazil. Right: Torrential rainfall lashes the Rio Japura in the central Amazon Basin. Facing page top: Floating vegetation soaks up the sunlight on a tributary of the Rio Japura. One traveler through the Amazon described such a scene as 'the river and the forest - it does not matter where, they are all monotonously alike'. Facing page bottom: Freshly cleared and burnt rain forest land in Brazil. Land cleared in this way remains fertile for only a few seasons before the few nutrients are exhausted.

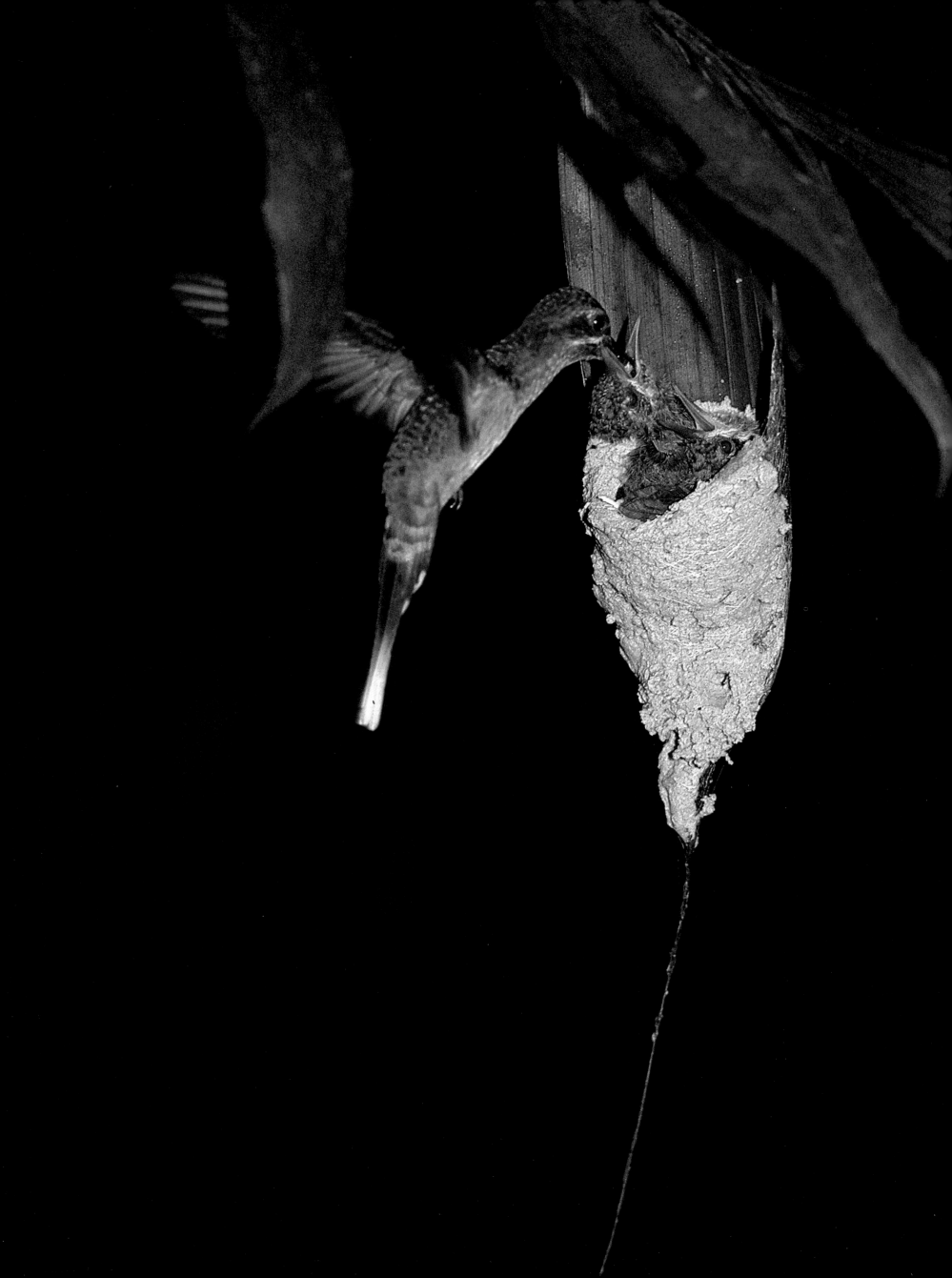

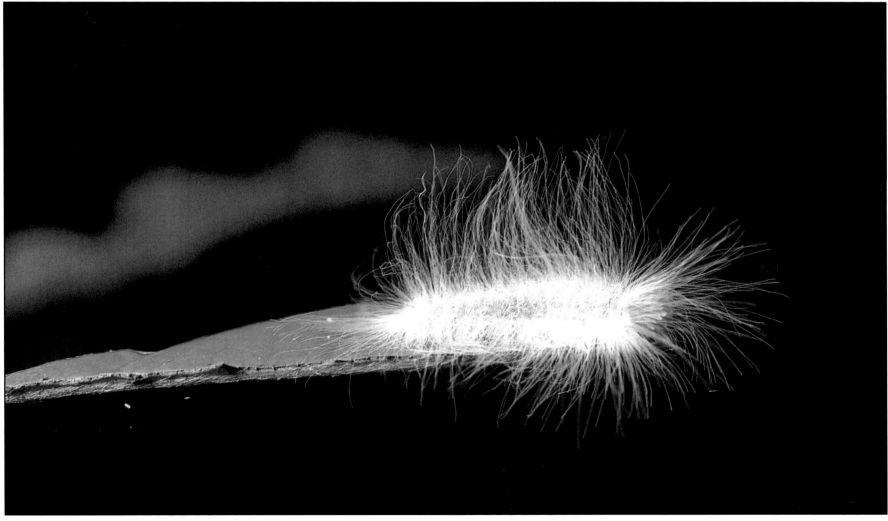

Facing page: A white-bearded hermit humming bird (Phaethornis hispidus) *hovers beside its tiny* nest while feeding its hungry young. Top: Apoica wasps constructing a nest on the underside of a branch in the Amazon Basin. Above: A hairy caterpillar feeding on a leaf. Overleaf: The mighty Iguacu Falls of southern Brazil. The falls are over 260 feet (80 meters) tall, twice the height of Niagara, and are divided into a number of steps and cataracts which make up the total spectacle of the falls. Rainfall in distant mountains is seasonal so the flow over the falls varies enormously. In some years the river dries up completely.

from the scientific programme.

It was not until many years later that the evidence was re-evaluated. By that time several other travelers had described meeting pairs of large, tail-less monkeys on the ground and various Indian stories confirming the existence of a ground monkey had been gathered together. Taking as the starting point the premise that de Loys had accurately reported what he had seen but had drawn the wrong conclusions, the scientists began work. It rapidly became clear that the size of the beast had been accurately stated. De Loys said it stood 5 feet 1 inch tall. The photograph of the creature included a crate known to be 18 inches tall. By comparing the two the scientists estimated the monkey to be 5 feet 3 inches tall, confirming de Loys' data.

Using the original data various possibilities were considered and rejected. The creature had only 32 teeth, which is unknown for American primates, but were common in African species. The creature is also different from South American monkeys in that it is said to move in pairs rather than in large troops. Finally it was decided that the most likely explanation was that de Loys had shot an unknown species of giant spider monkey which, for some reason, had lost its tail as a result of evolution.

Such a conclusion may be close to the truth, but has again been dismissed by the scientific world. This has refused to accept the existence of the creature until a specimen is brought out the forests. Meanwhile this fascinating creature may be facing extinction due to the destruction of its habitat. Nobody is studying this possiblity because, officially, the creature does not exist.

Other tales of creatures unrecognised by science have come out of the South American rain forests. There are tales of anacondas up to 100 feet (30 meters) long, three times the official maximum, which are reported to lurk in extensive swamps. In the Pando region of northern Bolivia, west of Riberalta, the locals occasionally report seeing a large four-legged beast with a long tail which lives in swamps but which leaves three-toed tracks when it ventures on to land. Exactly what this

might be is unknown, but similar tracks have been reported elsewhere. Reports of a large black cat were once dismissed as equally unlikely, but it is now known that the jaguar does occasionally occur in a totally black form.

More controversial are the tales of primitive men in the interior, particularly in the dense forests of the Matto Grosso. The earliest reputable witness to these beings was the explorer Percy Fawcett who traveled through this region in 1914. Passing through the territories of tribes never before visited by Europeans, Fawcett eventually came to the Maxubi who informed him that the next tribe, the Maricoxi, were savage cannibals little better than animals and could not be trusted. Undeterred Fawcett pushed on until he met the

Above: The feathery plumes of the Pseudobombax *flower which is pollinated exclusively by bats. Below left: An orchid of the* Cattleya *genus from northern Brazil. Below: A delicate pale orchid from the Amazon rain forest. Facing page: The multi-colored bloom of a helicona. Overleaf left: A blue and yellow macaw (Ara ararauna). Overleaf*

right: A red and green macaw (Ara chloroptera). The macaws are the birds perhaps most typical of the Amazon rain forest. They are loud, raucous, colorful and large, and so are easily spotted. They habitually fly some distance from roosts to feeding grounds, often crossing rivers in noisy groups of up to two dozen individuals.

Maricoxi. He came within a few paces of one before the arrows began to fly and the Europeans were obliged to retreat, shooting into the trees to frighten their attackers.

Fawcett described the Maricoxi as being covered in thick hair. The forehead sloped backward from pronounced eye-ridges and the eyes were small and round, very unlike those of the surrounding tribes. Other reports have been made since, all similar to those of Fawcett. Some naturalists believe that this indicates that Neanderthals, or some similar line of early humans live in the rain forests. Other scientists dismiss the tales as ridiculous.

The difficulty with many reports of unknown animals is that the version received by science is often very garbled and exaggerated. It can be difficult to credit the fact that an actual creature may lurk behind the stories. A fine example are the tales of a creature called the mapinguary. The forest tales describe the creature as a one-legged humanoid which hops through the forest and attacks anything it meets. The truth behind the stories are the circular prints placed one in front of the other with great regularity. Nobody has yet satisfactorily explained these odd tracks.

Whether or not the Amazonian rainforest contains such amazing creatures as tailless monkeys, giant snakes or massive swamp creatures, it certainly does contain a bewildering variety of wildlife which has been recognised by science. The heart of the entire rain forest is the great river and its tributaries and it is here that some of the most fascinating wildlife is to be found.

The Amazon rises high in the Andes mountains on the 17,000 foot (5,000 meter) slopes of Peru's Cerro Huagra not far from the Pacific Coast. From there it runs northward as a mountain stream, gathering the contents of other watercourses and becoming increasingly sedate. At Iquitos the river

Top: The red flowers of rain forest mistletoe (Psitticanthus). Above: A howler monkey makes a spectacular leap from one tree to the next. Glimpses such as this are all a traveller usually sees of these creatures. Left: A juvenile three-toed sloth (Bradypus tridactylus) in its habitual motionless pose in the Amazon rain forest. Right: A sunlit blossom in the valley of the Rio Japura. Facing page top: The lowland rain forest during the flood season when hundreds of square miles of forest are inundated. Facing page bottom: An afternoon downpour on the Rio Japura.

turns suddenly east, collects the Napo River and becomes the Amazon of the rainforest. From Iquitos to the ocean, many hundreds of miles to the east, the average slope is barely 1 inch per mile (20 millimeters per kilometer). This gradual slope gives the river its characteristic sluggish flow and gentle movements.

As the river flows eastward it moves through the dense growth of the rain forest, but the action of the river itself divides the forest into two distinct forms. Spreading out as much as 20 miles (35 kilometers) on either side of the river is the floodplain. This broad flat area is made up of lakes, side channels and forested lowlands. Beyond the floodplain the land rises to form permanently dry ground blanketed by rain forest. The forest of the floodplain is in many ways distinct from that of the higher ground. It is periodically flooded, often for several months each year, and has its own patterns of life.

The life cycle of the floodplains begins in

December when massive rainfall in the mountains causes the rivers to flood. The entire plain is inundated to a depth of many feet. The entire length of the Amazon and its many tributaries becomes a massive, slowly moving lake of water. The waters remain high for between four and eight months after which the ground re-emerges and the waters return to the river course. From this lake emerge the trees which may reach as high as 100 feet (30 meters) or more. Relatively few species of tree can tolerate the loss of oxygen to the roots which seasonal flooding involves, but those which can are adapted to the strange yearly cycle.

Among the most common trees in the floodplains are the rubber tree, which first brought Europeans to the Amazon rain forest in numbers, and the palms. Both rely on the flood waters to disperse their seeds, but in very different ways. The rubber tree produces vast numbers of seeds at the height of the floods. The nut-like seeds are produced in capsules which pop open in the heat of the sun, catapulting their contents some distance. The majority of seeds on each tree mature within a few days of each other, producing a regular shower of seeds. These drop into the water and drift away with the lazy current. When, some weeks later, the floods subside, the seeds come to rest on damp ground and germinate to produce new rubber trees.

Unfortunately for the rubber tree, the fish have a particular liking for its seeds. They can hear the sound of falling nuts from a fair distance and hurriedly congregate to feast on the nutritional seeds. One of the most common seed-eating fish is the tambaqui which grows to over 3 feet (1 meter)

Above: Rain clouds over the Rio Negro in Brazil. The Rio Negro gained its name, meaning 'black river' from the fact that its waters are stained dark with rotting vegetation in contrast to the pale muddy waters of the Amazon and most of its tributaries. Left: The dense foliage of the forest above the Amazon's floodplain. Facing page: The massive floating leaves of the waterlily Victoria amazonica *which may reach 6 feet (2 meters) in diameter. The large white flowers smell strongly of pineapples but only flower for one night before sinking to produce seeds. Overleaf left: A hyacinth macaw (*Anodorhyncus hyacinthinus*), one of the most beautiful but least often seen of the macaws. . Overleaf right: A toco toucan (*Ramphastos toco).*

These pages: The Rio Potaro throws itself into the Kaieteur Gorge forming one of the most spectacular waterfalls in the world. The river is over 300 feet (100 meters) broad where it tumbles over the edge of the 741 feet (225 meters) tall cliff. It was not until 1870 that a European pushed far enough inland along the Rio Potaro to discover the falls. Today, the mighty cascade lies at the center of a large national park in which the Guyana government has protected the wildlife and rain forest of the region. Left: A rectangular patch of young trees clearly shows where an Indian village had practised slash and burn agriculture for a few years.
Overleaf: The sluggish, muddy waters of a stream in the rain forest of Guyana.

in length. Large numbers of these fish invade the forest as the floods rise and gather round rubber trees to feed. The fish are equipped with tough, broad teeth which are capable of crushing the nut shells. During their weeks in the forest, the tambaqui feed voraciously on seeds until its body is loaded with enough fat reserves to last it through the thin times until the seeds are again falling.

Other trees do not rely on their seeds floating to suitable germinating ground but actively encourage fish to snap up the seeds. Palm nuts are surrounded by fleshy, nutritional pulp. When the seeds drop into the flood waters, the fruit floats. If left unmolested the seed behaves much as does that of the rubber tree. But more often fish spot the fruit and swallow it whole. The seed is protected by a special covering which stops it from being digested on its way through the intestines. When the fish defecates, usually some distance from the tree where the fruit was formed, the seed drops straight to the flooded forest floor. When the waters subside it germinates and begins the struggle upward towards the light.

The forest floods provide opportunities for other fish beside seed-eaters. The arowhana hunts

*Facing page: A king vulture (*Sareoramphus papa*) in Guyana. Unlike other vultures, the king has a highly developed sense of smell. The dense forest makes vision relatively unimportant for locating carion, so scent has become of greater*

importance. Above: A capybara, at 4 feet (1.3 meters) the largest living rodent. Below: A squirrel monkey. Below right: A beautifully marked ocelot. Bottom: A three-toed sloth. Overleaf: The hungry gaze of a jaguar.

take young mammals.

One of the largest fish in the rivers is the pirarucu which may grow to over 6 feet (2 meters) in length. It hunts other fish and has developed a complex breathing mechanism which aids its hunting. During the low water season many fish are concentrated in the rivers and streams where oxygen is often deficient. Starved of oxygen, the majority of fish become slow and sluggish. The pirarucu, however, is able to extract oxygen from the air and so remains active and able to hunt effectively.

Until the coming of the Europeans the pirarucu had no enemies. It was too powerful for the local tribesmen to hunt easily and too large to be eaten at a sitting. The introduction of steel spear points and salting made pirarucu hunting a viable proposition. The hunting of this fish for city dwellers is still a major basis of the fishing industry in the rain forest.

Larger still than the pirarucu and probably greater predators are the two species of dolphin which live in the Amazon. The larger of the species is the boutu which may grow up to 9 feet (2.7 meters) in length. It is generally recognised as being a rather primitive species of dolphin, but it is nonetheless highly successful. It hunts small fish voraciously and is the only creature capable of hunting the larger fish of the river. It is thought to hunt large prey by means of a disabling bite to the tail which halts any attempts at escape. Unlike marine dolphins, the boutu can move its head from side to side, a vital ability in the murky river

insects and is much the same size as the tambaqui. It has eyes divided into upper and lower halves. The upper half scans the surface of the water and is capable of seeing accurately some distance out of the water. The lower half of the eye searches the water beneath for potential danger and prey. Arowhana feed principally on insects and small birds which alight on the water surface, but they will also be more adventurous in finding food. They can leap anything up to 4 feet (1.2 meters) out of the water to pluck beetles and birds from overhanging branches. They have even been known to

waters.

The other species of dolphin in the Amazon is the tucuxi, closely related to marine dolphins. It is more advanced than the boutu but is less adapted to take advantage of the seasonal floods. Even at the height of the floods the tucuxi remain in the river channels. They appear to build up fat reserves during low water times to sustain them through the floods when their food moves into the forest.

It is in the dry forests that the majority of the wildlife commonly associated with the rain forest is

to be found. Insects of all types are present in enormous numbers and a bewildering variety of forms. Indeed, it has been tentatively estimated that many thousands of species exist in the Amazonian rainforest which have never been collected by scientists and remain unrecognised. The great mass of insects provides a readily available food supply for those mammals able to feed on them.

The tamandua or tree anteater is one of the most common of these. Growing to around 2 feet (60

These pages: The giant otter was once common throughout the rain forests of South America. Today it is much rarer due to extensive hunting for its valuable pelt. Though it is officially protected in many areas, hunting continues and the

creature is becoming increasingly rare. It spends much time in the waters hunting for fish, birds and other aquatic creatures. Measuring over 5 feet (1.6 metres) in length the giant otter has few natural enemies although the anaconda (facing page

bottom) is one. Overleaf left: The ornate hawk eagle (Spizaetus ornatus), one of the smallest and most agile birds of prey in the South American rain forests. Overleaf right: A spectacled owl (Pulsatrix perspicillata) which hunts small

mammals and other prey in the dim forest light.

centimeters) long the tamandua is a nocturnal creature rarely seen during daylight hours. It climbs easily through the trees with the aid of a prehensile tail, but is clumsy on the ground. It goes in search of termite nests, which it finds in hollow trees and in branch forks. Having found a nest, the tamandua uses the long, powerful claws on its front legs to tear open an entrance. As the termites scuttle forward to discover the origin of the damage, the tamandua flicks out its long, sticky tongue. Dozens of insects are scooped up with each flick and consumed.

Barely a quarter the size of the tamandua is the aptly named pygmy anteater. Found throughout the rain forest from southern Brazil to southern Mexico, the pygmy anteater concentrates more on ants than its larger cousin but otherwise lives in much the same way.

Two very similar slow-moving mammals of the rain forest are the sloths. Both the two-toed sloth and three-toed sloth live in the Amazonian rainforest, but the three-toed species is more common and has been more extensively studied. It is a most remarkable creature for not only does it live up to its slothful name, but it has evolved a remarkable lifestyle suited to its special surroundings.

The three-toed sloth spends most of its life hanging from tree branches. Its characteristic upside-down stance has led to some strange adaptations. The fur of the sloth is unique among mammals in that it lies from the belly to the back, rather than lying in the opposite direction. In this way the fur runs rainwater off the upper side of the animal efficiently and stops the creature becoming waterlogged.

The fur is also unusual in that it changes color with the seasons. The secret of the color change lies in the fur's structure for each hair is grooved and ridged. This creates an ideal habitat for algae which thrive. During damp weather the algae are green and match the surrounding foliage. During rare dry spells, however, the algae dries out at much the same rate as the trees and so the sloth becomes a wilting yellow shade for perfect camouf-

lage.

So efficient is the camouflage of the sloth that many go entirely unnoticed. They can hang motionless, appearing to be simply a clump of vegetation or hanging moss. It has been estimated that sloths are among the most successful rain forest mammals, in terms of numbers, but nobody is quite certain due to the difficulties of accurate counting.

Sloths spend about three quarters of the day sleeping. When awake they often remain motionless, or move extremely slowly. It has been estimated that the top speed of a sloth is around 1 mile per hour. Such speeds are only maintained

for a few minutes, after which the sloth relapses to torpidity. Occasionally a sloth will climb down to the ground and drag itself clumsily from one tree to another. On the ground the sloth is virtually helpless and can move at only around 200 meters (640 feet) per hour. Despite this the creatures sometimes undertake long journeys, thought to take place about once a year. When undertaking such marathons which may be as long as 8 kilometers (5 miles), the sloths not only cover open ground but will swim wide rivers with equanimity. The task of paddling across a stream many hundreds of meters wide does not deter the sloth, even though it may take several hours to accomplish.

Migrations apart, the social life of the sloths is poorly understood. They are seen most often singly, never in numbers larger than a pair. Most encounters between sloths are distinctly unfriendly. They resent coming across each other while feeding, as if jealous of food sources. When two meet on a branch they will often fight, using their long sharp claws to inflict serious injury on each other. Occasionally a sloth will be killed in one of

these contests, but death appears to be rare. This is not so much because of any lack of aggression, but simply because sloths are highly resilient to injury. Even the most serious of injuries will often heal completely within a short time.

The meat of the sloth was highly prized by the indigenous tribes of the Amazon, but it was a notoriously difficult creature to hunt. Not only was it difficult to locate because of its camouflage, but it was awkward to kill. Arrows or blowdarts could hit the creature fairly easily, if it was low enough in the branches, but the sloth was so firmly attached to the branch that it would not fall. Sloths maintain their tenacious grip with the aid of long, sharply hooked claws. Tribesmen eager to dine off sloth would have to clamber up the tree and along the branch to recover their kill.

The appearance of Europeans in the rainforest led to an unexpected effect on the sloths. The indigenous hunters soon noticed the impact effect of a rifle bullet on a victim. They would frequently beg a passing traveler to help them hunt sloths. The heavy bullet crashing into the sloth often dislodged it from its perch and brought it crashing to the forest floor from where it could easily be recovered.

If the flesh of the sloth was highly esteemed, its popularity was rivalled by that of the tapir, another mammal of the rainforest. One traveler pushing upstream in a large river canoe in the early 1930s was roused from a doze by his chief paddler who excitedly pushed a rifle into his hands and demanded that he shoot a group of tapir crossing the river. The somewhat bewildered man raised his rifle and shot three of the creatures. However, the tapirs were devoured by piranha before the canoe could come up with them. A few days later, however, the traveler managed to kill a tapir on dry land and pronounced the roasted flesh to be delicious.

The eagerness of the locals to persuade visiting

*Top: The pygmy anteater (*Cylcopes didactylus*). The creature rarely grows to more than 7 inches (18 centimetres) in length, though its tail may double this. It lives almost its entire life in the canopy, only coming to the ground to move from one tree to the next. It searches out the nests of ants and termites, themselves restricted to the canopy. Center: A brightly colored* Dendrobates leucomeles. *The markings inform would be predators of the noxious substance in the frog's skin. Above: A drab* Eleuthero dactylus. *Right: A boldly marked caterpillar.*

Left: The Sierra Nevada de Santa in northern Colombia. Below left: A pair of king vultures (Sarcoramphus papa) roosting in a tree beside the Amazon. Inhabiting the densest forest, the king vulture remains something of a mystery. Its breeding habits are unknown, nor is it certain how long the birds live. What is known is that they will actively hunt live prey as well as feed on carrion. Below: An adult and juvenile common iguana Iguana iguana) in their favorite habitat, forested wetlands. These reptiles may grow to over 6 feet (2 meters) long. Overleaf: (left) A common iguana and (right) an emerald tree boa (Boa caninus).

Europeans to shoot tapirs is also linked to the difficulty of hunting these creatures. Stone-tipped arrows and spears were incapable of inflicting fatal injuries on the creature, protected as it is by stout bristles and an exceptionally tough hide. In order to obtain the tasty flesh, the tribesmen needed to resort to stratagem.

During the tapirs' breeding season groups of hunters would imitate the whistling mating call of the tapir in order to lure one into the open. Once the quarry was in view, the hunters rushed forwards and tried to lasoo it around the neck. If a hunter was successful he was invariably pulled off his feet by the frightened tapir as it bolted back to cover. Other hunters would try to grab the trailing rope or to hurl themselves on their colleague as he was dragged across the ground. If enough men could secure a hold on the rope, the tapir was brought to a halt and could be despatched with repeated blows. If not, the tapir reached cover and snapped the rope. Such robust hunting techniques made for exciting and tumultuous adventures, but were far more strenuous and demanding than asking a visitor to use his rifle.

Tapirs are to be found throughout the Amazonian rainforest and the dense forests which reach northwards to Central America. Standing around 3 feet (1 meter) tall, the tapir is covered in a uniform

dark brown coat of bristles which protects it from the sharp thorns of the dense cover it prefers. It is by habit nocturnal, though it often ventures abroad during daylight hours, and is most at home in swamps or along river banks. It is often said that the tapir dives to the bottom of rivers in search of food, but the extent of its alleged ability to walk on river beds is uncertain. What is known is that the tapir feasts extensively on buds, shoots, leaves and even twigs which it rips from plants with its strong teeth and tusks.

The chief predator on the various mammals of the American rainforests is the jaguar, the famous spotted cat of the dense jungles. Standing about 3 feet (1 meter) tall at the shoulder, the jaguar is easily the most powerful cat in the Americas and few indigenous creatures can resist its attacks. The jaguar is chiefly a creature of the forest, and its hunting technique reflects this. The jaguar relies

upon getting close to prey before launching an attack for it cannot maintain high speed for more than a few seconds. Its squat limbs are, however, ideal for dealing savage blows and inflicting fatal wounds on victims. A swipe from the clawed fore feet is usually enough to disable a prey, which is then finished off with a neck bite.

Jaguars typically hunt their prey in the dense thickets of the rainforest and are adept at climbing into shrubs and trees which overhang waterholes or forest tracks. Here they await the passing of a suitable creature. The first a victim may know about the presence of the jaguar is when it drops to the attack. Jaguars will also inhabit more open ground and were formerly common on the open pampas of Argentina. There they would stalk prey through long grass, endeavoring to remain hidden until the last moment.

Jaguars rarely attack humans, preferring to avoid such dangerous prey even in areas where guns are not common. However, the ferocity and rapaciousness of the jaguar, called *el tigre*, is well known and almost legendary. Before the coming of Christianity the jaguar played an important role in the religious lives of the local peoples. In South America the jaguar was often revered as symbolic of the night, or of gods of the night or death.

The warlike Aztecs revered the jaguar as symbolic of their own bloodthirsty reputation and fighting qualities. The Aztec ruled an empire which embraced many subject tribes and was at almost continual warfare with neighboring states. One of the most important purposes of Aztec armies was to bring captives back to the capital for sacrifice to the sun god, at the rate of around 100 each day. Commanders were drawn from amongst the particularly brave and ingenious warriors. They were allowed to symbolize their bravery and rank by wearing costumes of jaguar skin. Those who had risen to the very highest ranks dressed in trousers and jackets of jaguar skin with a stuffed jaguar head as a headdress so that their faces stared out of the gaping jaws of the great cat. A fearsome uniform indeed.

Though an efficient and silent killer, the jaguar is

Top: The scarred trunk of the cinchona tree Its bark is harvested and used to produce quinine, an anti-malarial drug. Above: A typical riverside dwelling in the Peruvian rain forest. Above right: A river meanders through the Peruvian rain forest. Right: The head of a Amazon dolphin emerges from the murky waters. Facing page: flooded forest on the banks of the Amazon.

not as formidable a foe to man as might be supposed. There have long been Indians, known as *tigreros*, who specialize in despatching jaguars which have taken to stock raiding. Such men are highly regarded for they hunt the jaguar without guns, a skill demanding much training and practice. Stalking jaguars in the dense undergrowth common in some areas of the rainforest is not a task to be undertaken lightly.

The two essential pieces of equipment for the *tigrero* are a good dog and a strong spear. Usually working alone the *tigrero* visits the site of a recent kill by the jaguar and inspects the surrounding land to discover the jaguar's likely resting place. The dog is then used to locate the jaguar. If the cat is lying up in dense cover, the *tigrero* uses the dog and the spear to goad it into the open. There the battle begins. Jaguars are accustomed to creatures fleeing as soon as they become aware of the cat's presence. The behavior of the *tigrero* in standing up to the beast seems to disturb it. Its normal hunting pattern disrupted, it will circle the man,

hoping for an opening.

Eventually the cat will rush forward and spring for the throat. The *tigrero* must instantly bring the spear point up level with the jaguar's chest and at the same moment hurl himself forwards. The combined closing speeds of man and beast is enough to drive the spear deep into the jaguar. A particularly well-aimed thrust will kill the cat outright. More usually the cat takes some seconds

*Left: A red-faced uakari (*Cacajao rubicundus*). Below: A stream drifts through the rain forest near Iquitos, in Peru. Below left: Dawn breaks over the upper Amazon near Iquitos. Bottom: A woolly monkey (*Lagothrix lagothricha*), one of the fastest moving monkeys in the rain forest. Woolly monkeys live in troops of as many as 50 individuals. Facing page: A two-toed sloth (*Choloepus didactylus*) with its young clinging to its chest. The young stays with the mother for several months before moving off on its own. Overleaf: Trailing lianas and leaves emerge from morning mist in the rain forest of Venezuela's Henri Pittier National Park.*

to die. During this time the *tigrero* must take care to maintain a firm grip on the spear, while at the same time keeping clear of the flailing claws of the injured cat. This is the most dangerous time for the hunter and more than one has suffered serious and fatal wounds while attempting to keep the jaguar pinned to the ground.

Jaguars, unlike most cats, are fine swimmers and readily take to the water in search of prey or fresh hunting grounds. They are known to have a particular taste for certain types of fish. When the forests are flooded and fish move among the trees in search of seeds, the jaguars take large numbers. One of the cat's favorite tactics is to lie on a branch just a few inches above the water surface. It prefers a tree whose seeds are ripe and dropping

for fish are more common in those areas. As soon as a fish drifts within reach, the jaguar drops into the water to attack the fish, which may be half as large as itself.

This spectacular and unusual behavior is said to be even more cunning than it appears at first sight. It is rumored among local people that when resting on a branch, the jaguar will gently tap the water surface with the end of its tail. This imitates

the sound of seeds dropping into the water and lures fish to their deaths. It is unclear whether jaguars actually employ such a technique for the tale relies on anecdotal reports from non-experts.

The tree-climbing ability of the jaguar is of vital importance for its success as a hunter. The majority of animal life of the rain forest is to be found in the canopy, so the jaguar must be able to penetrate the higher branches to take advantage of the rich food source. Some of the jaguars favorite foods are the many species of monkey which

*Top: A beautiful blue morpho butterfly (*Morpho nestira*) from the rain forests around Yungas in Bolivia. Above: A drab dung-eating butterfly of the genus* Papilio *feeding on the forest floor near Yungas. Right: A pair of aptly named sulphur butterflies (*Phoebus sp.*) suck moisture from the riverside mud in Bolivia. Far right: A tiny* Actinote momina *butterfly from northern South America. Facing page top: The magnificent Hacha Falls formed as the Rio Carrao tumbles down from the Venezuelan highlands towards the coastal lowlands in the Canaima National Park. Facing page bottom: The moisture laden air of the rain forest turns to mist at dusk in Venezuela's Henri Pittier National Park. Overleaf left and right: Views in the forests of the Henri Pittier National Park.*

inhabit the upper branches. The great cat devours them in large numbers and is probably the major predator on the New World Primates.

The New World monkeys are a diverse group of creatures, but share several general characteristics. Their faces tend to be flat and their nostrils placed far apart. The fur is very thick and has a woolly, rather than hairy, texture. The tails tend to be rather long and are very muscular. They are prehensile, meaning that they can be used to grip branches as a fifth limb when climbing. The four limbs are slim and capable of agile movement. The hind feet tend to be better at gripping than the fore limbs which are used more for manipulating food than movement. The general result is that New World monkeys are exceptionally fine climbers highly adept at moving at speed through the upper branches.

Of the thirty-odd species of monkey found in the great South American forests, the most vociferous and therefore most noticeable are the aptly named

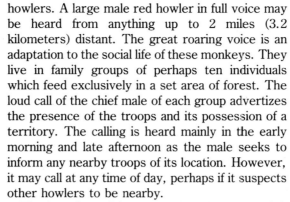

howlers. A large male red howler in full voice may be heard from anything up to 2 miles (3.2 kilometers) distant. The great roaring voice is an adaptation to the social life of these monkeys. They live in family groups of perhaps ten individuals which feed exclusively in a set area of forest. The loud call of the chief male of each group advertizes the presence of the troops and its possession of a territory. The calling is heard mainly in the early morning and late afternoon as the male seeks to inform any nearby troops of its location. However, it may call at any time of day, perhaps if it suspects other howlers to be nearby.

The booming call is produced by the male which has a highly specialized throat mechanism. The larynx is large, and hollow being expanded into the form of a trumpet. When the monkey calls, the larynx moves up and down in the throat.

The howlers are the largest monkeys of the Amazon rainforest. A large male may reach 3 feet (90 centimeters) in length and weigh as much as a large dog. Like most South American monkeys they feed almost exclusively on leaves though they may take some fruits. There are three distinct species of howler, the red, the black and the Guatemalan. The latter is limited to chill highland forests of Central America, but the other two species are widely distributed through the rain-

Above: A ginger flowers in the Napo River country of Ecuador. Right: The blooms of a mountain bomaria in Ecuador. Far right: A purple Helicona. *Below: A sobralia orchid. Facing page top: Rain sparkles on the petals of a green orchid. Facing page bottom: A red and green* Helicona. *Overleaf: (main picture left) upland rain forest in Ecuador; (main picture right) a dramatic waterfall near Baeza, Ecuador; (top left) a harmless grasshopper; (top right)* Dendrobates histrionicus, *used by local tribesmen to make arrow poison; (bottom left) urticating caterpillar and (bottom right) A bird eating spider.*

forest. They are distinguished chiefly by their color. The black howler is jet black, but the red howler is not necessarily red. Females and young tend to be yellowish in hue with only adult males showing the russet shades. Even they are not always red for it would seem that a complete drenching turns the fur yellowish in hue.

More nimble in the trees are the spider monkeys, several species of which range widely through the forests. The largest is the black spider monkey whose range extends northward from the Amazon to the basins of the Orinoco and other rivers. Spider monkeys have long tails which are strong enough to support their entire weight, allowing them to dangle from branches to reach succulent but otherwise inaccessible pieces of fruit. The underside of the tail tip is bare of fur and heavily ridged so as to provide a firmer grip on branches. As with other New World monkeys the black spider monkey lives in family troops and has a fairly well defined home territory.

Perhaps the most unusual of the Amazon monkeys in appearance is the bald uakari which is restricted to the Amazon forests close to the foothills of the Andes. This medium-sized monkey is around 2 feet (60 centimeters) in length and lacks the long prehensile tail of other species. It lives in the trees in isolated pockets and is comparatively rare even where it is to be found. The most remarkable feature of this monkey and other

uakaris is on the head and face. These are entirely bare of fur and have a characteristic pink tinge. When the monkey becomes excited or frightened, the bald face becomes flushed and takes on a bright red color.

Much smaller than the normal run of New World monkeys are the marmosets and tamarins. These little creatures are rarely more than a foot (30 centimeters) in length, though they often sport tails which can more than double this measurement. They are highly active creatures, which are often seen scampering along the tops of branches and leaping from bough to bough, but are incapable of swinging beneath branches and lack prehensile tails. They are characterized by tufts of hair on their faces which seem to be used in social displays.

Across the Atlantic Ocean another massive stretch of rainforest has a particular and diverse primate fauna every bit as varied and fascinating as that of the Amazon and neighboring American rainforests. The African rainforest is in many ways much the same as that in the Americas. It has a similar climate with year round rainfall and equable temperatures.

Like the South American forests, those of Africa are centered around a vast river basin, in this case that of the Congo. The Congo Basin covers over 1 million square miles (4 million square kilometers) making it second only to that of the Amazon.

Bounded to the south and east by tall mountains and to the north and west by plateaux, the Congo basin has only one small opening through which the Congo River flows to the Atlantic. The bulk of the basin lies over 1,000 feet (300 meters) above sea level and is covered by dense rainforest or vast stretches of swamp and marsh. The belt of rainforest reaches northwestward from the Congo Basin to run along the coast of West Africa as far as Senegal. Fringing the true rainforest throughout its range is a thick belt of tropical forest which shares many animal and plant species with the rainforest, but lacks the equable climate and features distinct seasons.

The primate wildlife of this extensive stretch of forest is, if anything, more diverse than that of the New World rainforests. The most impressive

Top: The small piranha subject of many blood-chilling tales.
Above: A green-throated hummingbird.
Right: A yellow rumped cacique (Cacicus cela), a fruit-eating bird usually found in large groups. Facing page top: A blue-tailed emerald hummingbird (Chlorostilbon mellisucus) feeding its chicks. Facing page bottom: The Napo River in Ecuador.

These pages: Butterflies from the Ecuadorian rainforest. Facing page: (top left) genus Ithomiidae; (top right) a clearwing butterfly (Cithaerias menander); (bottom left) a heliconid; (bottom right) a blue butterfly. Left: Genus Ithomiidae. Below and bottom left: A coolie butterfly (Anartia amathea). Bottom right: An Heliconius melpomene. Overleaf: (top left) flooded forest in the Cuyabeno Lagoon in Ecuador; (bottom left) sunset in northeast Ecuador; (right) aerial roots trail from trees near Baeza in Ecuador.

primate of all is the gorilla which inhabits the upland forests where ferns and bamboo are common. The gorilla is without doubt the largest and most impressive of the primates. A large male can stand well over 6 feet (2 meters) tall and weigh in excess of 600 pounds (280 kilogrammes).

Such an impressive size has inevitably given rise to stories of the gorillas' savagery, tales which have been easier to believe because of the gorilla's behavior. When disturbed or angered, the gorilla is likely to indulge in an impressive and frightening threat display. Rearing on to his hind legs the male will beat his chest with his fists to produce a loud booming noise. Returning to all fours, it will dash forwards screaming loudly and shaking bushes and undergrowth in a savage display of strength. These alarming displays may be enough to frighten off intruders. If not, the gorilla may flee into cover, or it may launch a real attack, assaulting the cause of

its alarm with powerful blows and fatal bites.

The tribesmen who inhabit the home range of the gorilla have learnt to respect the large ape. Before the advent of rifles in the area, the gorilla was a very real danger. A man armed with a spear could not be certain of the outcome of a clash with a gorilla. Tales of organized assault by gorillas were told, but evidence for such attacks is scarce. It is said that bands of gorillas will sweep down out of the forests and sack entire villages. It is said that the men and children are killed by the angry apes, while the women are carried off to the forests. Such stories are now rare, as is the gorilla, but continue to surface. In the mid-1980s a local woman returned home in tears to report that she had been assaulted and raped by a large male gorilla. The locals believed the story, but scientists dismissed it out of hand.

Much has been made recently of the docility of the gorilla and it is true that they have a well organized and peaceful social life. They live in family groups of around a dozen individuals, though groupings of thirty individuals have been reported. Each clan is dominated by an adult male with

Left: A cattle egret (Ardeola ibis) *in Madagascar. This bird is widespread in both the Old and the New Worlds and frequents open land as well as forested wetlands. It preys on fish and insects, which it snaps up in its spear-like bill. Below and below left: The ring-tailed lemur* (Lemur catta). *This is possibly the best known of the 27 lemurs for it takes readily to captivity and breeds well. In the wild, the ring-tailed lemurs live in bands of up to 50 individuals and feed on the fruits and leaves of the trees which they inhabit.*

Though some scientists have managed to integrate themselves with gorilla troops and have been able to approach the beasts very closely, the animals should always be treated with respect. If they feel threatened or become suspicious they can quickly turn aggressive.

The chimpanzee is another ape to inhabit the African rainforests. Smaller than the gorilla, the chimpanzee is still some 5 feet (1.6 meters) tall when it stands erect and may exhibit similarly aggressive behavior when disturbed. Like the gorilla, however, the chimpanzee spends most of its time in peaceful social groups. Chimpanzee troops characteristically lack a dominant male and may be made up of almost any mix of males, females and young. They take more readily to trees than the gorillas, probably because they are much smaller and more able to scamper through the canopy. They feed on fruits, nuts, leaves and other plant material, but will also take eggs and insects. Chimpanzees have also been seen to hunt

silver fur on his back. It is this male which leads the group on its continual wandering search for food and which defends it against intruders. The silver-back, as the dominant male is known, maintains his rule throughout his life. Only when he dies do the younger males of the group fight each other for dominance.

Gorillas are vegetarians which feed on leaves, fruits, bark and buds. They are often encountered in bamboo thickets where they feast on young shoots. Young individuals and females may climb

trees in search of food, but the males are too heavy to do so and find their food on the ground. The troop rests at night in nests which they build out of foliage from surrounding bushes. Waking at dawn, the creatures spread out to feed during the cool of early morning. As the heat of noon approaches, the gorillas gather together and rest until the temperature drops. Then they feed again, moving on in apparently aimless fashion until dusk gathers. Building fresh nests, the gorillas retire for the night.

small mammals, killing the prey by smashing them against a stone or tree trunk.

Like several other creatures of the African rainforest, the chimpanzee has extended its range to the surrounding tropical forests and even out on to the grassy savannah. The troops which inhabit the more open landscapes have developed different habits than their forest counterparts. They tend to live in groups more obviously centered around the family of a dominant male and rarely take to trees, even when they are present.

Living deep within the rainforest of the central Congo Basin is a distinct type of chimpanzee known as the pygmy chimpanzee. As its name suggests this species is about half the size of a normal chimpanzee, but is otherwise very similar. It shares similar foods and social structures with the chimpanzee and is regarded by some scientists as simply a sub-species.

The forests of Liberia shelter another pygmy version of a well-known animal. The pygmy hippopotamus is found near water through much of West Africa, but it does not spend its days in rivers as does its larger counterpart. Indeed, the pygmy hippopotamus is anatomically and behaviorally quite distinct from the standard hippopotamus and is placed in a separate genus. It has longer legs and a smaller head in proportion to the body and is a solitary animal which defends its feed territory against rivals. The hippopotamus, by contrast, gathers in herds led by an old male.

The question of other pygmy creatures in the African rain forest is a difficult one. There is some evidence to suggest that miniature versions of several creatures have evolved to live in the dense forests. The forested uplands of Cameroon are inhabited by tribes which still live a similar life to that led before European colonization. These peoples have frequently told of a strange animal which outsiders have likened to a rhinoceros, but one which is much smaller than those of the open savannah. No outsider has yet seen the purported forest rhinoceros, nor brought back any hard evidence, but several people who know the region are prepared to admit that some sort of large mammal might inhabit the unexplored forests.

Similar uncertainty surrounds the dwarf elephant alleged to inhabit dense forest north of the Congo River. Unlike the rhinoceros, the existence of small elephants is beyond doubt. However, science refuses to accept them as a distinct type but considers the specimens obtained to be merely juveniles or freaks. Local tribesmen told the

*Top right: a female black lemur (*Lemur macaco*) with its young clinging to its belly. Above: A pair of Indris (*Indri indri*), the largest of the lemurs. Growing to around 28 inches (70 centimetres) in length, the indri gave rise to tales of hairy, dog-faced men when Europeans first visited Madagascar. Top left:*

*The aye-aye (*Daubentonia madagascariensis*) which is restricted to Madagascar's dwindling rain forests. It preys on wood boring insects which it extracts with its long fingers. Left: A red-ruffed lemur (*Lemur variegatus ruber*).*

Above: A group of villagers at the rain forest village of Kambama in Sierra Leone. The simple dug out canoe is their only connection with the outside world. Right: A pygmy hippopotamus (Choeropsis liberiensis) from Nigeria rests in weed covered waters. Below: The umbrella tree of West Africa, the fruits of which are devoured in large quantities by monkeys. Facing page top: Forest crowds the banks of the Moa River in Sierra Leone. Facing page bottom: An impenetrable thicket of bamboo in the rain forest near Tiwai in Sierra Leone.

earliest explorers of a type of river elephant no taller than a man, but it was not until early this century that one was shot and its remains brought to civilization. The specimen was declared to be a young elephant by those scientists who inspected it.

Not long afterward a live individual was recovered and taken to New York zoo where it lived for some months. It was only 6 feet (2 meters) tall though was clearly of some age. This specimen was labelled a freak dwarf by scientists. That there are small elephants in the African rain forest is beyond doubt, but their scientific status remains in considerable dispute.

The existence of creatures unknown to science may appear somewhat surprising in central Africa, but it is not impossible that dwarf forms of known animals have developed to suit life in the dense forest. Much more disturbing is the possibility of a giant creature of a type utterly unrecognized by science. Yet persistent stories from the Congo point to just this possibility.

Tribesmen who live around the great swamps which fill the heart of the rainforest basin have consistently reported a creature known by various names, but often termed the *mokele mbembe*. According to those who claim to have seen it, this creature is a giant reptile slightly smaller than an elephant which lives in the swamps. It is said to have a long neck and tail, and a small head.

Although extremely dangerous and likely to attack anything which disturbs it, the *mokele mbembe* is said to eat aquatic plants and to excavate a resting place in the shoreline.

Exactly what type of a creature this might be is unknown. In 1980 a team of American scientists pushed up river to try to find out. They came back without any firm evidence, but having spoken to many locals who claimed to have seen the creature. The descriptions they gathered were remarkably consistent, causing the Americans to state that they believed that a large, unknown animal did exist in the depths of the forests.

That relatively large creatures can remain unrecognized by science even in areas supposedly well explored is shown by the story of the discovery of the okapi. Throughout the mid and late 19th century tales came out of the Congo of a type of forest horse called okapi which was partially striped like a zebra and ate leaves. In general the tales were disbelieved, even by those Belgian officials who lived in the rainforest and administered the area for the colonial government.

Sir Henry Johnston, a British officer from neighboring Uganda, decided to take up the quest and, in 1900, penetrated into the forest accompanied by pygmy guides who showed him tracks of the mysterious okapi, but failed to catch one for him. Undeterred Sir Henry wrote to various official posts in the Congo asking for all information to be sent on to him. A few months later two skulls and a skin arrived at his station. He at once realized that the creature was not a horse at all. He thought it was more like a giraffe and sent the remains to

*Facing page: The Victoria Falls where the Zambezi River hurls itself 350 feet (170 meters) into a gorge. Top: A heavily buttressed tree stands in Zambia's Mushishama Botanical Reserve. Above: A juvenile lowland gorilla. Right: A silverback mountain gorilla (*Gorilla gorilla beringei*). Far right: A young mountain gorilla. Overleaf: (left) A chimpanzee (*Pan troglodytes*) and (right) a lowland gorilla.*

London for inspection.

The scientists, who had long disbelieved the stories, were now convinced and decided that the okapi was indeed a relative of the giraffe. They gave it the scientific name *Okapia johnstoni* in honor of the man who proved its existence.

Though now accepted as real, the okapi is not very well known because of its secretive habits. It lives in the densest thickets of the Congo rainforest where it feeds on the leaves and shoots of trees and bushes. Like the giraffe, the okapi has a long and mobile tongue which it uses to grasp foliage and pull it into the mouth. So long is the tongue that it is used to clean the face, including the eyes. The okapi stands over 6 feet (2 meters) tall at the shoulder, but lacks the long neck of the giraffe, its cousin. The shy creature lives alone, only being found in pairs during the breeding season. It flees from other creatures, which would explain why it remained unknown for so long.

At the other end of the scale of size is the equally retiring water chevrotain found throughout the African rainforest. This tiny deer is barely 2 feet (85 centimeters) long which enables it to squeeze into the densest brush in search of a hiding place. The nimble legs of the water chevrotain ensure that it can scamper across the forest floor with amazing agility. But it is in the water that the creature shows its finest movements. The creature swims easily and, when startled, will dive for the muddy bottom in order to elude pursuers. It feeds chiefly on land, seeking out fruits and grass, but has been seen to take fish and crustaceans in the lakes and rivers. The curious little animal is generally regarded as a type of deer, but may be related to the pigs.

No doubt exists concerning the largest of the aquatic mammals of the African rainforests, the hippopotamus. The hippopotamus is quite clearly in a family of its own, although it is widely recognized as being related to the pigs and peccaries. The creature is found exclusively in the larger rivers and lakes of Africa, though it is widely distributed beyond the rainforest areas.

The presence of the hippopotamus caused great problems to the geographers of antiquity. For centuries the only part of the known world where the hippopotamus lived was the Nile, so it was assumed that they were confined to this river. When, therefore, traders returned from West Africa with tales of rivers abounding in hippopotamus the geographers were puzzled. They tried to solve the problem by attempting to draw the Nile such that it looped far to the west before flowing through Egypt. Later expeditions sent out by the Roman Emperor Nero pushed up the Nile and showed that no such loop existed. The geog-

These pages: Eastern lowland gorillas in Zaire's Kahuzi Biega National Park. Strenuous efforts are made to safeguard both the gorillas and their habitat, but poachers continue to kill the apes. Left: A silverback at rest in the noonday heat. Top: A silverback warily regards the intruding photographer. Above: A silverback gives a threat display before retreating into dense cover. Facing page: females and young feeding on vines. Overleaf: A leopard lurks in a tree. Leopards often rest in the branches, and may pounce on unwary creatures passing beneath. Leopards take a greater proportion of their prey at night than other big cats.

*The tiger (*Panthera tigris*) is the largest hunter of the rainforests, reaching over 11 feet (3.3 metres) in length. It may feed on any mammal in the Asian rain forest, except adult elephants, but prefers chital and other deer when available. A few tigers prey on humans as well as on more normal quarry. Such confirmed maneaters, rather than tigers which kill when disturbed, can be extremely dangerous. One tiger active before the First World War killed and ate over 400 people before it was shot by a British officer named Jim Corbett. Facing page: The leopard (*Panthera pardus*).*

raphers gave up trying to make sense of the reports and marked down the anomaly on their maps.

In fact the hippopotamus is a highly successful mammal which plays a vital role in the environment of the African forests. A fully grown male is a big animal, weighing up to 4 tons and standing some 5 feet (1.7 meters) at the shoulder. On land the hippopotamus appears somewhat ungainly. Its stumpy legs hold its barrel-shaped body only a few inches above the ground and it seems to move only with great effort. In the water, however, it becomes graceful. The water supports most of the creature's weight, enabling it to swim or run on the river bed with great ease and speed. It is hardly surprising that the hippopotamus spends most of its time in the water, where it finds refuge from the burning African sun.

When night falls, however, the hippopotamus emerges from the water in search of food. It browses on various types of vegetation but seems to prefer grasses. It finds young crops almost irresistible and this has led to animosity towards the hippopotamus among local farmers. In the past

Top: A spoonbill (Platgalea leuxorodia) with chick in Sri Lanka. The spoonbill swings its bill from side to side in the muddy waters of rainforest streams, filtering the thick liquid in search of crustaceans and other minute animals. Left: A painted stork (Ibis leucocephallus)

preening itself. Above: A spider of the genus Cynapes. Facing page top: a trio of painted storks perch on their evening roosts before settling down for the night. Facing page bottom: A painted stork accompanied by a flock of ibises at Bharatpur in India.

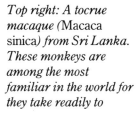

Top right: A tocrue macaque (Macaca sinica) *from Sri Lanka. These monkeys are among the most familiar in the world for they take readily to captivity and have been kept as pets. The leopard* Panthera pardus *is the most widely spread rain forest hunter, being found in both Asiatic and African forests. Leopards will feed on almost any type of prey, as well as on carrion.*

Overleaf: An evening view of a lake in the Gal Oya National Park in Sri Lanka. Facing page: A brown headed barbet. Left: A female purple sunbird (Cinnyris asiatica) feeding her young. Below: A male purple sunbird displays his plumage in the sunlight. Bottom: A paradise flycatcher (Terpsiphone paradisi).

the hippopotamus was regarded as a welcome source of meat for local tribesmen. The flesh is deep red in color and rather like beef in texture, though much gamier in flavor.

Traditional methods of hunting hippopotamus varied widely. In some areas the tribesmen engaged in the hazardous business of spearing hippopotamuses from dug-out canoes. The creatures were first harpooned with long spears to which were attached skin floats which marked the position of the injured creature. Once sufficiently weakened, the creature was finished off with spears. When first killed, the hippopotamus invariably sank to the river bed, but within 5 hours the putrifying stomach contents created enough gas to cause the carcass to float. The body was then boarded by a pair of men who paddled it to the shore.

Elsewhere less adventurous techniques were used. Where rivers were relatively narrow lines of stakes were driven in above and below small herds as well as along the banks. The caged creatures were then despatched at leisure by thrown spears and the meat cured for storage. Traps were also sometimes set. These consisted of trip wires on known hippopotamus routes connected to suspended spear heads backed by massive weights. A traveling Englishman had the misfortune to encounter such a trap in the 1880s. "My horse's feet struck the line attached to the weighted spearhead," he wrote. "Down it came, just missing my head and entering the horse close behind the saddle." The horse was killed instantly.

Such predation by man had little effect on the overall population of hippopotamuses, but in recent years a more potent incentive has been added to the hunting of these large water creatures, money. The adults have canine teeth enlarged into tusks which may be nearly 2 feet (60 centimeters) long and weigh anything up to 7 pounds (3.5 kilogrammes). The ivory each of these yields fetches a high price on the open market. The ease with which hippopotamuses may be shot with high powered guns has led to their extinction in many areas.

As early as 1901 the future of the hippopotamus was seriously in doubt. Frederick Courteney Selous was a famous British big game hunter who shot for sport and also for science. He fought in the Matabele Wars of the 1890s and was killed taking part in the conquest of German colonies during World War I. Like many hunters, Selous was determined to ensure conservation so that there were animals to shoot, and so he deplored the

slaughter. He predicted the rapid extinction of the hippopotamus, but suggested that "if the indiscriminate killing of hippopotamuses by either white men or natives and the cruel custom of firing at the heads of these creatures from the decks of river steamers be put a stop to, I believe that this most

Though it takes its name from the Nile river, the creature is found in nearly every body of water of any size in Africa. In the lakes and streams of the rainforest lurks another species of crocodile which is much less known to science than the Nile crocodile. This is the West African dwarf crocodile

which rarely reaches more than 5 feet (1.6 meters) in length. Apart from the fact that it is extremely rare, little is known about this creature. It might prey on fish more than does its larger cousin.

Though a savage hunter, the Nile crocodile is perhaps the best parent of the reptile world. Most

interesting animal will long outlive other large animals." He added that in his opinion "when these animals have been banished from an African river by the progress of civilization, that river has lost one of its highest charms and greatest ornaments."

Many people have agreed with Selous since and today the hippopotamus is protected across most of its range. Only in well-managed game parks do they survive in numbers, perhaps they are most frequent in South Africa. Outside protected areas, the hippopotamus survives only in small numbers and frequents inaccessible swamps and lakes.

If the hippopotamus is the great vegetarian of the African rivers, the dominant hunter is undoubtedly the crocodile. These large reptiles are well adapted to life in the water. They have webbed feet and long, flattened tails to provide power for swimming. They will readily take fish, but the main ingredient of the diet is thought to be birds and mammals. The prey is taken when it comes to water to drink. The crocodiles lurk just beneath the surface. Only their eyes and nostrils project above the water. Gradually the crocodile paddles itself towards the intended prey. In a final rush the reptile lunges forward, jaws agape in an attempt to seize its victim. If the crocodile manages to grasp the prey in its teeth, it drags it quickly into deeper water and holds it beneath the surface until it drowns.

Having secured a kill, the crocodile may swallow it whole if possible. If not, the crocodile will securely lodge the carcass beneath a rock or log. Grasping a limb in its mouth, the reptile spins itself in the water. This tears loose a piece of flesh which can be bolted whole, the crocodile being incapable of chewing. Occasionally, the carcass is left for several days so that decomposition sets in and the flesh becomes softer and more easily dismembered.

The characteristic crocodile of Africa is the Nile crocodile, one of the largest species in the world.

*Above left: A Ceylon hawk eagle (*Spiaetus cirrhatus ceylanensis*) in the Wilpattu National Park in Sri Lanka. Above: A Malabar pied hornbill (*Anthracoceros coronatus*). The precise purpose of its extraordinary bill is obscure. Left: An Indian darter (*Anhinga melanogaster*). This agile swimmer hunts fish beneath the water surface and, unlike other fishing birds, it captures prey by spearing rather than by gripping. The fish is flicked into the air to remove it from the end of the beak. Facing page: A Ceylon serpent eagle (*Spilornis cheela*). Serpent eagles are found in forests from Southern China to Pakistan, and vary considerably in different locations. It hunts by leaping from a perch, rather than by diving from the sky, and prefers lizards and snakes to other prey. The talons are rough and serrated to provide a better grip on such slithery victims.*

Facing page: Two views of the Kinabatangan River in Malaysia's Sabah province. This river suffers periodical flooding and is often clogged by silt, both the result of logging. Clearing the rainforest in the mountains where the river rises causes the soil to erode and the water to run off with great speed. Above: Rain forest on Borneo, which is rapidly being cleared. Left: Raw rubber dripping from a rubber tree in Sabah. Far left: Hanging pitcher plants in the forests on the slopes of Mt Kinabalu in Sabah. Insects are trapped in the pitchers and digested.

reptiles lay their eggs, often bury them, and then abandon them to their fate. Nile crocodiles, however, behave in a very different way. The 50 or so eggs are buried deeply in sand close to open water. For three months the mother remains in the area, frequently visiting the site of her camouflaged nest.

After some 12 weeks, the eggs hatch out and the buried young call loudly. Hearing this noise the mother hurriedly digs her young free of the sand or mud and carefully carry them in her mouth to a nursery previously selected. Usually this is a sheltered waterside spot protected by overhanging undergrowth. At first the young feed on insects, later progressing to small fish and birds. During this time the mother ensures that her young remain within sight and defends them against predators. After about 6 months the mother appears to lose interest and wanders off. Left to their own devices, the young scatter and lead independent lives.

Beyond the rivers and swamps which dominate so much of the landscape, the African rain forests are outwardly very similar to those of the Amazon.

*Far left: A giant ginger growing on the banks of the Niah River on Borneo. Above: A bird's nest fern. Left: A rhinoceros hornbill. Facing page: (top left) a pair of long-tailed macaques (*Macaca fascicularis*); (top right) a stump-tailed macaque (*Macaca arctoides*); (below left) clustered stems of the spiny palm (*Eleiodoxa conferta*) in the Bako National Park in Sarawak; (below center) an infant silvered langur (*Presbytis cristata*); (below right) a delicate waterfall in Sarawak's Lambir National Park.*

The trees grow tall and straight to a canopy some 100 feet (30 meters) above the ground. In the humid, sunlit canopy grow a wild profusion of flowers, parasitic plants and creepers. It is in the canopy that the majority of plants and animals live.

One of the most curious birds of the region is the African harrier hawk. Outwardly built like many other hawks, the African harrier hawk sports a handsome grey plumage with black tail and wing tips and a barred chest. The bird spends relatively little time flying, preferring to clamber along branches and flutter between perches. It does this

in its constant search for its favored food, the chicks of other species. Finding a nest, the African harrier hawk mercilessly drives the parents away and then devours the chicks. Some prey species have developed nesting techniques designed to defeat predators such as the African harrier hawk. Weaver birds construct elaborate nests which hang beneath branches, while others lay their eggs in holes within the tree. Unfortunately, the African harrier hawk can cope with both with its amazing agility. Able to dangle beneath branches by one leg and twist around, the hawk then uses its beak and

free talon to secure its prey.

Equally unusual in its feeding habits is the palm-nut vulture, which is the only vulture to exclude meat almost entirely from its diet. Instead the bird concentrates on the seeds of oil palm trees. This vulture is found only where the oil palm is common and rarely moves far from its home. The bird gathers the palm seeds and perches on a frond where it uses its beak and talons to strip the highly nutritional husk from the seed. The husk having been consumed, the seed is discarded and falls to the ground. This helps the oil palm to

and predominantly green in color, though the underside is blue and the throat carries a red flash. The head is decorated with a black tuft of feathers and a cluster of white bristles.

Equally retiring is the nicator, a dark green bird which lives in the understorey of foliage and hunts insects. Though inconspicuous and shy, the nicator often betrays its presence by suddenly breaking out into a loud and prolonged chattering song.

Sharing the rainforest with the magnificent variety of birds and mammals are a number of reptiles. Of these perhaps the best known are the chameleons. These lizards are highly specialized for their life of insect eating and have brought stalking to a fine art. The two eyes of the chameleon are able to move independently of each other. With this unique ability, the chameleon can scan the surrounding branches for potential victims.

When moving through the foliage, the chameleons employ a slow, steady gait which is interrupted with swaying motions to mimic the gentle movements of twigs and leaves. This disguised approach blends the lizard into its surroundings and enables it to approach a victim with little chance of being seen. The camouflage is greatly helped by the lizards ability to change color. This ability has been exaggerated by some, but the chameleon is

spread for the seed may be dropped some distance from the parent plant.

Rather more colorful is the Congo peacock, a bird restricted to the densest sections of rainforest. Because of its inaccessible home territory and secretive habits, the Congo peacock did not become known to science until 1936 when a specimen was brought out of the forests. Even today it has rarely been seen by scientists and most information about it comes from local tribesmen. It is reported that the birds are invariably found in pairs and that they feed on fruits. Apparently the pairs stay together for life and build a nest of twigs in tall trees. The plumage of the birds is, as its name suggests, colorful though it is not as spectacular as that of the Indian peacock. The Congo peacock is over 2 feet (60 centimeters) long

certainly able to change hue in order to match its surroundings.

Once a victim is located, the two eyes swivel forwards to focus on it and judge its distance. The chameleon creeps towards the victim until it comes within range for the use of its remarkable tongue. This organ enables the chameleon to catch its prey with almost incredible accuracy and speed. The tip of the tongue is coated in a sticky secretion which entraps any insect it touches. The 'firing' mechanism consists of hinged bones in the mouth to push the tongue out and powerful circular muscles within the tongue itself. Together these are capable of extending the tongue to twice the length of the lizard's body. Any insect unfortunate enough to be struck by the adhesive tongue is doomed for it is rapidly pulled back into the mouth and swallowed.

Above: A Malay fishing owl (Ketupa ketupa)*. Right: A lesser adjutant stork* (Leptoptilos jaranicus)*. Adjutant storks were named by European soldiers who* *likened the bird's still gait to that of regimental officers. Below: A flying frog* (Rhacophorus sp.)*. Flying frogs have large, splayed feet which can* *be opened out to form gliding 'wings'. Facing page: A praying mantis.*

The entire attack, from the opening of the mouth to the jaws clamping on the prey may be over in less than a tenth of a second.

Until comparatively recently the vast expanses of rain forest in West and Central Africa were completely unknown to outsiders. Even today, there are extensive tracts of forest which no human other than local tribesmen have trod and which have been mapped only with the aid of satellites. One of the first Europeans to penetrate

the great forests had the name of Mungo Park and was employed by the British Association for Promoting the Discovery of the Interior Parts of Africa. Park's first attempt was reckoned by contemporaries to have had poor chances of success. Two earlier explorers had already died on their journeys before penetrating far beyond civilization.

Park, however, was undaunted and set off in 1795 up the Gambia. After several weeks of hard

traveling, Mungo Park reached the upper Niger, but was captured by a local tribal king, robbed of everything he owned and his servants sold into slavery. He did, however, succeed in escaping and made his way to the territory of a neighboring king who was persuaded to donate supplies. Several months later Park stumbled out of the rainforest. Despite serious illness, Park wrote up his notes and maps, sending them back to London.

In 1805 Mungo Park returned with a large

expedition of 44 Europeans and a train of carriers. He marched rapidly to the upper Niger where he built a river boat with the intention of cruising downstream to the Atlantic. Notes and maps made to date were sent back to civilization with part of the team while Park and his companions set off downstream. They never reached the Atlantic. Those who did not succumb to virulent rainforest fevers were finished off by local tribesmen.

Other explorers followed, to be met by death or success in equal measure, but it was not until 1877 that the great Congo river was traveled for the first time. The honor went to the American Henry Stanley. After finding Dr Livingston in the interior, Stanley returned to civilization before setting out on another expedition aimed at discovering the outlet of the mysterious Lualaba River which rose in the interior and flowed northwards. Assembling a boat on the upper Lualaba, Stanley set off downstream accompanied by 17 canoes and over 300 men. For more than 2,000 miles (3,200 kilometers) the craft were rowed and paddled downstream. Rapids and whirlpools destroyed more than half the canoes while disease and hostile tribesmen accounted for all but 120 of the men. Finally, nearly three years after leaving Zanzibar, Stanley cruised into a European trading station. He

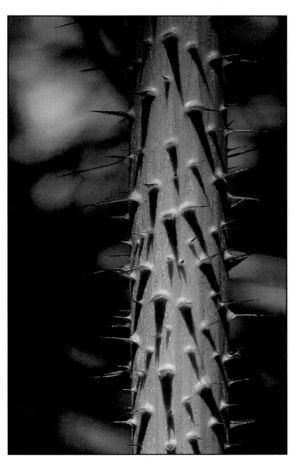

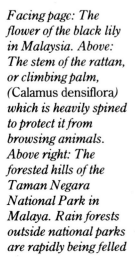

Facing page: The flower of the black lily in Malaysia. Above: The stem of the rattan, or climbing palm, (Calamus densiflora) which is heavily spined to protect it from browsing animals. Above right: The forested hills of the Taman Negara National Park in Malaya. Rain forests outside national parks are rapidly being felled

and cleared. Top left: A showy sobralia orchid from Malaya's Cameron Highlands. Top right: Fulgoroid plant hoppers on a young fern frond.

discovered that he was on the Congo. Stanley returned to the rain forest in 1887 where he was subjected to a vicious attack by pygmy tribesmen and again lost most of his companions.

Travel through the great forests is today somewhat safer, but no less troublesome. The officials of various governments and occasional rebel movements which hide out in the rain forests are often suspicious of foreign travelers. Minor formalities may delay the traveler as a procrastinating official attempts to discover the true reason for the journey. In regions wracked by civil war and crime such precautions are understandable, though many travelers find a small bribe overcomes the objections of even the most suspicious official.

The great African rain forests have their own

particular perils for the traveler. Of these the most endemic are malaria and bilharzia. The former is transmitted by mosquitos which carry the tiny blood parasites from one person to the next. Bilharzia is more insidious and difficult to counteract. The tiny parasite which causes the disease is to be found in most rain forest rivers and streams. It burrows into the skin on contact and quickly affects the nervous system. The general effect is one of lethargy and, eventually, death.

Hookworm is rather more common but fortunately less severe in its effects. It is found in mud and stagnant pools of water. If a person steps into an infested pool, the hookworms latch on to the skin and drill their way into the flesh. The parasites cause much discomfort and, like the sututu of the

Amazon, are difficult to remove. Added to torment by these creatures is the constant discomfort of hot and humid conditions in which scratches and sores take far longer to heal than normal.

The leopard is perhaps a more obvious natural hazard to those traveling through the dense rain forest. Though the great cat usually shuns humans, it has been known to take to maneating. It is often thought that the key to this behavior is the liking of leopards for dog flesh. Many leopards have been seen to enter rainforest villages in search of small dogs to eat. It is presumed that on such forays a leopard may be surprised by a human and kill in self defence. Having gained a taste for human flesh, the leopard may take to maneating as a way of life. Such events are fortunately rare but maneating leopards can be particularly voracious. One beast was credited with over 300 human kills before a British hunter shot it.

*These pages: The siamang (*Hylobates syndactylus*). This large gibbon is able to swing from branch to branch or run along boughs with equal speed. They are often found in family groups, with the offspring of a couple sharing its range for several years. The siamang feeds principally on fruit, but will consume leaves and insects. Above and right: A young male. Far right: An adult holding a baby and a juvenile. Top right: A family group. Facing page: Female with young. Overleaf: the Cicenter River on Java.*

a wide variety of prey including monkeys, antelope, birds, fish and even snakes. Small prey are consumed on the spot, but larger carcasses will be dragged to cover, often on to tree branches. Here the leopard feasts at will, often dozing between feeds. A large prey may be watched over and fed on for several hours.

The leopard has one of the most beautiful coats of any animal. The cat is marked by dark roseate spots which vary from chocolate brown to black. The background color of the coat also varies from

night. In India such black leopards are termed panthers and are greatly feared. They are held to be voracious stock raiders and to possess almost supernatural powers.

The leopard is arguably the most successful of the big cats for it is widespread across the Old World. Before the spread of agriculture and persecution by cattle herders, the leopard was to be found throughout Africa from Cairo to the Cape and right across southern Asia to the Pacific Ocean. It roamed far to the north of the range of other rain forest animals, penetrating into the Siberian forests.

Sharing the Asiatic section of this range was the largest cat of all, the tiger. Reaching over 13 feet (4 meters) including the tail, the tiger is an immensely powerful animal capable of subduing any beast

Reaching well over 10 feet (3 meters) in length, including the tail, the leopard is the Old World equivalent of the jaguar. Not only does the spotted skin give a visual similarity, but the two cats lead very similar lives. The leopard is unable to maintain a chase for long and relies on stealth and stalking to gain prey. Like the jaguar it has relatively short but powerful limbs and both climbs and swims well. In the normal course of events, the leopard will attack almost clear white to a deep nut brown. The differences are generally recognised as being regional and have led to some authorities identifying several subspecies within the leopard species. Throughout its range the leopard occasionally produces completely black forms. These individuals are particularly handsome and are said to be highly skilled at nocturnal hunting when their black coat blends into the pitch dark of the rain forest

Left: A sonneratia flower opening at dusk on Rakata Island, Indonesia. Bottom left: A black pomatocalpa orchid from Java. Bottom right: A chloranthum orchid from Sumatra. Facing page: The orchid Bulbophyllum macranthum *from Indonesia. Overleaf: Some of the birdlife of the Indonesian rain forests: (left) A blue-eared kingfisher (*Alcedo meninting*); (top right) a colorful male wreathed hornbill (*Rhyticeros undulatus*); (bottom right) a great billed heron (*Ardea sumatrana*).*

*Left: A spider on its nest with a fly held securely before being eaten. Spiders are major predators of the vast numbers of insects which inhabit the Indonesian rain forests. Right: Weaver ants (*Oecophylla smaragdina*) beginning to build a nest by pulling leaves together and joining them with tough strands of silky material. Below right: The colorful caterpillar of the thosea butterfly. Below left: A paper wasp (*Polistes*) constructing its fragile nest out of wood pulp. Facing page top: An atlas moth (*Attacus atlas*) rests on its cocoon while its wings expand and harden ready for flight. Facing page bottom: A two-horn rhino beetle (*Scarabaeidae dynastinae*). Overleaf: Monsoon rains lash the Cagenter River on Java. Unlike other rain forest areas, Indonesia has seasonal rainfall patterns. From October to April, heavy rain storms occur nearly every day. Even the 'dry' season the weather is wetter than in most areas of the world.*

which shares its range, excepting only the elephant. As with other rain forest hunters, the tiger stalks its prey and relies on surprise for success.

Sometimes a tiger will lie beside a jungle track or watering hole in the hope of ambushing a victim, but more often it moves in search of prey. Each tiger has a clearly defined territory within which it hunts. Males tend to cover several hundred square miles of forest and keep other males out of their hunting grounds. Tigresses, by contrast, have smaller overlapping territories and may share large kills.

When patrolling in search of prey, the tiger moves with a long, steady gait which covers much ground in a short period of time. As soon as it senses something of interest, the tiger stops to inspect it. If it turns out to be a potential meal, the tiger drops into a crouching position and begins the stalk. Generally speaking a tiger prefers to close to within 70 feet (20 meters) of a victim before launching an attack, but it may lunge from further if there is not enough cover. Once it has broken cover, the tiger bounds forward at high speed. It aims to spring at the prey, bowling it over and clamping the jaws around the neck in a grip which is often capable of breaking the neck instantly.

Once a kill has been made, the tiger drags its

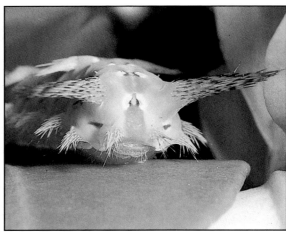

victim to cover where it can be consumed at will. Often a tiger will leave a carcass under cover and return to it each night until the flesh is consumed. The tiger seems unconcerned by the putrification which sets in. Even maggot-infested flesh will be munched with apparent relish. This habit of returning to a kill was formerly exploited by tiger hunters who would establish themselves in a tree overlooking a kill and shoot the tiger when it returned for a nocturnal feast.

Though the best-known tigers are those of India, the great cats have extended their range eastwards

through Indo-China to any region covered by forest. They have even established themselves on the islands of Indonesia where distinct subspecies have evolved. Both Java and Sumatra have their own recognised subspecies which are more lightly built and smaller than the Indian tiger. Island tigers are rarely more than 8 feet (1.6 meters) in length. The even smaller Bali tiger is now probably extinct.

The dense rain forests which extend throughout the Indo-China peninsula and through to the island of Indonesia and the Philippines are distinctly different in character from those of South America

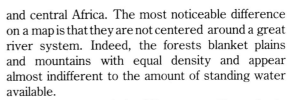

and central Africa. The most noticeable difference on a map is that they are not centered around a great river system. Indeed, the forests blanket plains and mountains with equal density and appear almost indifferent to the amount of standing water available.

The plant growth is different too. Not only do the rain forests of Southeast Asia contain completely different plant species from the great

*Right: A blue-throated bee-eater (*Merops viridis*) from Java. Left: A female wreathed hornbill (*Rhyticeros undulatus*). Below: A charming rufous-backed kingfisher (*Ceyx rufidorsus*). Above: A jumping spider (*Hyllus sp.*). Facing page: A view across the extensively forested mountains of the interior of Bali. The tiny island is a Hindu outpost in Moslem Indonesia. Overleaf: (left) a stem of pink orchids (*Erika moluccana*) and (right) a ladies slipper orchid (*Glaucophyllum*).*

forests of Africa and the Amazon, but they grow in entirely different patterns. At a height of around 100 feet (30 meters) there is a canopy of sorts, but it is not the dense layer of other rain forests. The canopy here is more like that of a northern deciduous forest being open enough to allow large amounts of light through to the forest floor.

Combined with the heat and humidity this light leads to a stupendous growth of ground level plants. The undergrowth of an Asian rain forest equates to many people's concept of a true jungle. There is rampant growth which makes travel virtually impossible except along cleared routes. In its natural state such forest can be penetrated only by using elephant walks or by arduous cutting with a machete.

The wildlife is quite distinct too. Not only is the tiger the dominant hunter, rather than the leopard, but the range of birds, mammals and reptiles is unique. The island nature of much of the forest has led to divergent evolution and nowhere is this more spectacular than on New Guinea. Itself a large island, New Guinea is riven into deep valleys and

high mountains which preclude travel and competition between species, even those which occur within a few miles of each other.

Descriptions of the birds of paradise must dominate any account of the wildlife of the island because of their beauty and variety. According to scientific classification the birds of paradise are high up on the evolutionary scale being rather advanced perching birds, themselves reckoned as the most advanced order of birds. But it is the glorious plumage of the species which endear them to the public.

Living as they do in dense forest and undergrowth, the birds of paradise need to be able to locate each other at mating time and to recognise members of their own species. The plumage has evolved to aid this. Only the males are bedecked in the gaudy feathers, the females being uniformly dull brown. The males of each species have an individual pattern of feather. The king bird of paradise is scarlet with a white belly and trailing tail feathers adorned with green end tufts. The King of Saxony's bird of paradise is gold and black and sports two trailing feathers at the back of the head which are longer than its entire body. The blue bird of paradise has taken display a step further by hanging upside down from branches and swinging backwards and forwards with its wings spread and tail feathers dangling.

The brilliant plumage of the males is only in evidence during the breeding season. At other

*These pages: The orang utan (*Pongo pygmaeus) *inhabits the dense rain forests of Borneo and Sumatra and may grow up to 5 feet (1.6 metres) tall. Though it is large and heavy, the orang utan is a tree dweller, moving easily through the canopy of the rain forest. It moves by brachiation, swinging beneath branches, though it never moves as fast as the more agile monkeys. When on the ground, the orang utan walks rather clumsily on all fours. Its main food is the vast array of fruits found year-round in the rain forest, but leaves, eggs and even small animals may be taken if the opportunity arises. Male orang utans tend to live alone, except during the mating season, but females may be found in pairs or small groups together with juveniles. At dusk, the apes construct a nest of twigs high in a tree and sleep until morning.*

times of year the birds are almost as drab as their mates. Feeding on insects, lizards and fruit, the birds are rarely seen except during the breeding season.

Though the great forests of Southeast Asia are so different from those of the Amazon in many ways, they are very similar in another. When Europeans began arriving in numbers the locals told them stories of strange monsters and ruined cities located in the forests. Unlike similar tales in the Amazon Basin, these have since been proved to be at least partially true.

First to emerge from the realms of legend were the lost cities. The first tales to filter out of the rainforest were recorded by missionaries in the 17th century. One of them, named Pere Chevreuil, even claimed to have reached the ruins and to have wandered along deserted and overgrown streets lined by massive temples, but few believed him. Other vague reports were made over the years, but the European authorities in the area were too busy establishing diplomatic relations or fighting wars to take them seriously.

Then, in 1861, a French naturalist named Henri Mouhot traveled up the Mekong and past the Tonle Sap Lake in search of new insects in which the rain forest abounds. While pursuing insects through the dense undergrowth, Mouhot was staggered to find himself suddenly confronted by a towering statue of Buddha some 20 feet (6 meters) tall. Hacking his way through the creepers and bushes, Mouhot found more statues, stone roads and tall walls. Pushing further he found a massive temple dominated by five lotus-bud towers over 100 feet (30 meters) tall. Abandoning his insect hunt, Mouhot returned to civilization with his story.

This time the lost city was taken seriously and

teams of scientists set off into the rain forest to study the ruins. After years of jungle clearance and excavation, the scientists have revealed the full extent of the lost city. It was immense. Conservative estimates suggested that it could have housed a population of over a million humans. Attached to the city was a spreading temple complex containing some 600 shrines and a major central temple surrounded by a moat over 200 feet (60 meters) wide.

Around the city and temples were huge artificial lakes, the two largest of which were over 4 miles (6 kilometers) long and one mile (1.6 kilometers) wide. At the center of each was a tiny island temple. Clearly the city had been the center of a vast area of cleared rain forest irrigated by complex water engineering. The great paddy fields so created would have supported vast numbers of people and allowed the construction of the city.

The city was named Angkor Thom and the

Top, above and left: One of only two Asian rhinoceroses with a single horn, the Javan rhinoceros was once found throughout Java and mainland Malaysia. Centuries of uncontrolled hunting and forest clearing have reduced its range dramatically. Today only a few hundred survive in a reserve on the western end of Java.

The creature was formerly hunted for its horn which is reputed to have medicinal properties. Poachers are still active, but official protection has reduced their activities. Facing page top: The banks of the Cigenter River in Ujung Kulon on Java. Facing page bottom: A heavy downpour deluges the Cigenter River on Java.

temple complex Angkor Wat, but their essential mystery remained. Nobody seemed to know what they were nor who had built them.

After much research and archaeological excavation historians finally identified the ruins as the capital of the Khmer Empire which had flourished from the 9th century onwards. For several centuries after its foundation, the Khmer Empire enjoyed uninterrupted success and steady expansion. New territories were conquered and surrounding kingdoms became tributaries to the mighty emperors living in Angkor Thom. In the 15th century, however, the Khmer state came into conflict with the rapidly expanding Siamese kingdom to the northwest. The records of the conflict were kept by the Siamese, whose country is now called Thailand. A series of wars were fought which culminated in a seige of Angkor Thom in 1431. For seven months the Siamese army camped outside the walls until it broke in and pillaged the city. Treasures were stolen and houses looted before the Siamese returned home with their spoils.

The following year the Siamese mobilized again, determined to complete the destruction of Khmer power by wiping out the royal family and killing or enslaving the entire population. But when they reached Angkor Thom, it was deserted. The hundreds of thousands of people had vanished and were never found. Careful historical study later revealed that a mysterious king accompanied by

numerous people established the city of Phnom Penh some time around 1435. It is widely suspected that Pohea Yat and his people were the remnants of the Khmer who had fled southwards to escape the Siamese.

As the fabled lost cities were yielding up their mysteries, the tales of large, savage reptiles which roamed the island jungles in search of prey remained unbelieved. Then, in 1912, a pioneering aviator flying across the Sunda Straits developed engine trouble and was forced to make a crash landing on the nearest island. For some days the intrepid airman wandered around the island before finding a settlement. During these days he came across a gigantic reptile which was feasting on a carcass. When he told his story, of course, virtually nobody took him seriously.

Fortunately one man did, a Dutch naturalist named Major Ouwens who was working in the area. He took the tale seriously and set out to investigate. He was rewarded by a 7 foot skin bought from a local fisherman who assured him that it was a small specimen of the 'land crocodile'. A few months later a live specimen was brought back by a team of zoological hunters. It measured 9 feet 6 inches (2.9 meters) and was dubbed the Komodo dragon after the island where it was captured.

These interesting beasts have been much studied since. They are a giant species of monitor lizard, smaller forms of which are common

Facing page: The Cibodas Waterfall on Java. Top: A mock viper rears up in imitation of a poisonous snake about to strike in order to deter a would-be predator. Above: A python lying coiled in a brakish water hole waits for a suitable prey to pass. Left: A golden tree snake draped around a bare branch. Overleaf: Dense forest foliage crowds the banks of a river in central Java.

throughout Australia, Asia and Africa. Like other monitors it is a hunter but due to its size scorns the insects and lizards which content its cousins. Instead the komodo dragon preys on pigs, buffalo and deer. Though it is a solitary animal, Komodo dragons will gather together at a large kill and tear the carcass to pieces with their strong teeth and powerful jaws.

Though the existence of the giant killer reptile has been proven, the tales of the little hairy men remain far from verified. The stories of this curious creature come chiefly from Sumatra where it is called orang pendek, meaning 'little man'. The vast majority of reports of this creature come from the depths of the rain forest and are made by local farmers or tribesmen. Only rarely do outsiders with some credibility in the eyes of science come across the beast.

The most complete description of the orang

Left: A delicate orchid (Vanda limbata). Below: An orchid on Sumatra (Arundina bambusifolia). Bottom: A Trichoglottis bipenicillata *orchid from Kalimantan in Indonesia. Facing page: The ghostly blooms of the orchid* Phalaenopsis ambilis. *Overleaf left: A strangler fig with its stems wrapped tightly around a supporting tree. Overleaf top right: A flock of flying foxes leaving their roost in the early morning. Overleaf bottom right: Cigenter River, Java.*

pendek was made by a Dutch forestry official named Van Herwaarden who worked in Sumatra during the 1920s. The Dutchman came across the female creature when searching for a new logging site. The creature leapt into a tree when it saw Van Herwaarden and clung to the trunk. Van Herwaarden studied it for some time and described it as being about 5 feet (1.6 meters) tall and very human in shape. The body was covered in dark brown fur though long shaggy hair fell down from the head to below the shoulders. The face was more human than ape-like though it had large canine teeth and a receding chin. Van Herwaarden realised that other similar creatures were in the vicinity when the creature gave a 'hoo-hoo' call and was answered from nearby. Van Herwaarden tried to climb into the tree to gain a closer look, but the creature leapt to the ground and ran off on its hind legs.

Other reports have been made over the years and all agree as to the same basic features of the orang pendek. Despite this series of reports, no specimen has ever been captured or shot so the very existence of the orang pendek remains in doubt. Even those convinced of their reality dispute whether they are a type of human or a form of ape.

Similar doubt surrounds the Tasaday of the Philippines. It is not that there is any doubt that this tribe exists or that they are human. These facts can be established by anyone who cares to visit them in their remote highland home. The dispute centers around their cultural origins and development.

In 1971 the Philippine government announced the discovery of the Tasaday tribe. It was said that the tribe had never before had contact with

Top: The colorful flower spike of the Helliconia collinsiana. Above left: The tiny yellow blooms of the Sumatran orchid (Dendrobium acerosum). Left: The purple funnel-shaped flower of the orchid Dendrobium anosmum. Above: The spectacular, many-petalled flower of the wild ginger plant (Phaeomeria speciosa). It was in search of spice plants such as this that Europeans first came to the East Indies. Facing page: A delicate orchid from the Moluccas Islands of Indonesia (Dendrobium strattotes). Overleaf left: The still waters of the sluggish Cigenter River in the Ujung Kulon region of Java. Overleaf right: A view into a deep gorge clothed in rain forest.

Europeans, nor with local farmers. They were claimed to be completely ignorant of farming and to have been separated from the rest of human culture for centuries, if not millennia. Numbering barely 30, the tribe lived in caves in a remote region, spoke a strange language and used tools unlike any known in the area.

A select number of anthropologists were invited to study the Tasaday and their findings startled the world. It was confirmed that the Tasaday were a stone age tribe which had lived in total isolation until recent logging operations had led to contact with the outside world. The culture of the tribe was extremely primitive but well suited to the rain forest environment. More specialists were called in to evaluate the language, customs and legends of the tribe. Soon afterwards the area was closed to loggers and scientists alike by the government which claimed to be concerned about the tribe and the local rain forest.

Years later the government was overthrown and an anthropologist hurried to the remote valley of the Tasaday to continue studies. He found a tribe of perfectly normal locals living in a standard Philippine mountain village happily farming their land. They told him that they had been paid by the former government to dress up and behave like stone age people. The entire affair had been a hoax. Scientists involved in the original investigation were unconvinced. They maintained that their tests were so stringent that there had been no

possibility of error. A new expedition to the tribe brought out the information that the Tasaday were a genuinely primitive people who had misled the new investigator because they were frightened about their future.

The entire Tasaday affair remains unresolved with learned experts disputing evidence and findings with each other. Only the Tasaday themselves know the truth. But since they persist in giving conflicting stories little can be gained from them. As many earlier explorers have found to their cost, unsophisticated rain forest people often tell strangers anything that will keep them happy. It is a form of politeness.

The confusion surrounding both the Tasaday and the orang pendek is indicative of the great changes occuring in the rain forests of the world. For millions upon millions of years, the rain forests have remained virtually unchanged. The monotonous climate of year round heat and humidity has continued to provide virtually ideal conditions for rapid growth, death and renewal.

In this environment species have been free to evolve and proliferate in bewildering variety. Thousands of species of plants and animals developed to suit the conditions of the rain forest. Many species are so specialized that they are found only in a few square miles of forest, or in connection with another species on which they are totally dependent.

This magnificent and varied environment is now

Top: The flower stalk of the orchid Pholidota imbricata. *Left: The large red flower of the wild ginger plant (*Phaeomeria speciosa*). Most ginger used in the kitchens of the world today is produced by cultivated plants which are grown in open fields, cleared of rain forest. Above: The delicate white blooms of the orchid* Coelogyne peltastes. *Small flowers like this can be easily overlooked amid the dense foliage of the rain forest, but are among the most attractive plants of the forest. Facing page: The blooms of the Sumatran orchid.*

under serious threat. It is not some cataclysmic natural upheaval, such as an ice age or drought, which is threatening destruction. It is human activity causing the damage. Already many thousands of square miles of prime rain forest have been destroyed and vast areas are felled each year.

Of course the rain forests have been exploited on a limited level for centuries. Slash and burn agriculture kept many thousands of people in the rain forest. They would fell a patch of forest, grow crops for a few years until the thin soil was exhausted and then move on. The abandoned field would slowly regenerated into mature rain forest. Likewise local populations felled trees, dragging them out of the forest for use as timber. Such low-level exploitation did little environmental damage for it was on a scale that allowed the rain forest to regenerate itself.

However, the 20th century has seen an increase in the pace of rain forest development. A traveler passing through Riberalta in the southern Amazon in the 1930s was amazed to find a sizeable town where a few years earlier there had been only a few grass huts belonging to rubber tappers. He also discovered isolated farms and outposts on rivers which had before been lined by unbroken vegetation. By the 1950s the pace of change was increasing beyond measure. Whereas previously exploitation had been principally by local people for local people, the outside world now began to take an interest in the rain forest.

The most obvious attraction of the rain forest is timber. Rain forest trees such as mahogany and

Top left: A maiden's veil stinkhorn fungus (Dictyophora sp.*) from the forested highlands of Papua New Guinea. Far left: Epiphytes growing in the rain forest of Papua New Guinea. Left: Wasps swarming over the leaf behind which they have* *built their nest. Above: A web spider of the genus* Argiope *waits for a prey to stumble into its trap in the forests of New Guinea. Facing page: The magnificent blooms of the flame-of-the-forest (*Mucuna novaeguineensis*).*

Left: A common
blossom bat
(Syconictris crassus
sleeping on its roost.
Above: A colorful
caterpillar from New
Guinea. The shape of
the caterpillar disguises
its true shape. Below
left: A praying mantis
awaits a victim in New
Guinea. Mantises hunt
with their front legs
which can be shot out to
grasp passing insects
with incredible speed.
Below: A leaf-eating
grasshopper rests on a
twig in the rain forest.

Facing page: A
voracious giant wood
spider (Nehila
maculata) with a
tettigonid prey on its
web.

ebony yeild hard tough timber which is not only
beautiful but is useful for a variety of purposes. The
felling of large commercially valuable trees was and
remains a highly profitable business. Large
acreages are cleared each year. The forest which is
thus cleared has little chance to recover for it is
destroyed over vast areas to which the distant
surrounding forest cannot spread seeds or animals.
Furthermore the land is rarely left alone. In some
areas, peasants move in to farm the thin soil.
Elsewhere cattle are grazed on the land producing
wide expanses of grassland. In a few places where
minerals are found large open cast mines are dug.
One such mine in the Amazon is over 15 miles (24
kilometers) across.

The clearing of the forests is made more
attractive by the fact that most of the nations
where rain forest occurs are extremely poor. The
rain forest is a valuable natural resource which can
be readily converted into foreign currency to
purchase much needed industrial goods and to
finance internal developments. Several governments view their rain forest as little more than a
cash bank from which withdrawals can be made at
will. At least one government has made it illegal to

criticise logging companies and others which fell the rain forest.

During the 1970s and 80s increasing concern at the rate the rain forests were being destroyed began to be voiced. People in many developed countries realized the tremendous damage being done to the environment and to the species of animal which lived in the great forests. The growing unease manifested itself in books, magazine articles and television programmes. These in turn alerted others to what was occuring and led to a snowball effect of public opinion.

Before long the opinion that something should be done to halt the destruction was being openly voiced. The problem, of course, was to decide what action should be taken. Some organizations began discouraging people from using rain forest products. This has been partially successful with the UK's consumption of South American cat skins slumping from 76,000 in 1975 to 34,000 in 1985. This, however, left the basic problem unsolved. The governments of rain forest nations were still short of money and continued felling timber to gain it.

Perhaps more encouraging has been the decision by some funds and charities to buy up large tracts of rain forest. These are then managed sensibly following long established forest management techniques to produce a steady, sustainable income without destroying the rain forest and its species. It has been shown that, in the long run, rain forest managed in this way produces four times as much money as if it were cleared for farming or ranching. Such schemes are still in their infancy compared to the large scale clearing operations, but they are making progress.

It is to be hoped that governments and industry can be convinced that keeping the rain forests is preferable to destroying them before these natural resources are lost to us forever. Once the rain forests have been destroyed it will be impossible to resurrect them and the many and varied plants and animals which inhabit them.

Top: The heavily forested hills and valleys of the almost inaccessible Northwest Highlands of Papua New Guinea. Above: A fig tree in the New Guinea rain forest.

Above left: A dense growth of vine bamboo which is typical of recently disturbed areas of rain forest in New Guinea. Facing page: Markham River country of New Guinea.

INDEX OF PHOTOGRAPHERS